SPECTAMUR

CW01498039

1ST BATTALION
THE EAST LANCASHIRE REGIMENT
AUGUST AND SEPTEMBER, 1914

BY

Captain E. C. HOPKINSON, M.C.

PRIVATELY PRINTED

SPECTAMUR AGENDO

Officers of the Battalion on Embarkation.

Back Row—2nd Lt. SALT, 2nd Lt. PARKER, Lt. HUGHES, Lt. MACMULLEN, Capt. GOLDIE, Lieut. DELMEGE, Lt. DYER, Lt. DOWLING, Lt. LEESON, Lt. CANTON, 2nd Lt. TOSSWILL.

Middle Row—[Capt. WALKER, A.S.C.], Capt. COVENTRY, Capt. CLAYHILLS, Lt. BELCHIER, Maj. LAMBERT, Lt.-Col. LE MARCHANT, Maj. COLLINS, Maj. GREEN, Capt. SEABROOKE, Lt. Q.-M. LONGSTAFF.

Front Row—2nd Lt. WADE, Lt. RICHARDS, 2nd Lt. HOOPER, 2nd Lt. MATHEWS, Lt. HOPKINSON, Lt. CHISHOLM, Lt. FLOOD, R.A.M.C.

Preface

Every effort has been made to make this record as accurate as possible but, as the information available has often been fragmentary and in some cases even contradictory, I am aware that errors may have crept in. In almost every case the information, very naturally, has related to isolated actions and the recollections of individuals and it has been no light task to piece together the patchwork in order to present a connected and balanced picture of the whole. If injustice has been done to any, whether by sins of commission or omission, I can only apologise and plead the difficulty of the task.

I wish to thank Lieut.-Col. J. E. Green, D.S.O., for a large part of the narrative and especially for his ever ready help and valuable criticism ; Capt. H. T. MacMullen, M.C., for much information and for his help in reconstructing " the old days" when motoring over the ground with me; the Historical Section, Imperial Defence Committee, for allowing me access to such records as threw light, often unfortunately rather dimly, on the situation.

E. C. HOPKINSON.

EDWINSTOWE,
  CHAUCER ROAD,
    CAMBRIDGE. 1926.

Contents

List of Illustrations

MAPS

PHOTOGRAPHS

Spectamur Agendo

In 1913 the author was sitting at the orderly room table as acting adjutant. The telephone rang and he was told that a large case was being sent to him and was to be deposited unopened in the mobilization store. It was to be signed for as " a case said to be maps." The case arrived, and was duly deposited in store and remained there unopened till August, 1914. That the maps it was then found to contain were those actually required for most of the fighting of 1914 is some proof of the efficiency of the General Staff. The Battalion, it is true, often lacked maps, but this was due to circumstances which could hardly be foreseen. That the British Army should have to retreat to Paris can scarcely have appeared probable, or that the IVth Division should so hurriedly be sent from the overseas base to the front, so that maps for reason of their sheer bulk were not always available at the right moment can hardly be brought as a criticism on those who had worked for the preparation of the Army for war.

For years before 1914 there lay in the safe in the orderly room a file of papers—the mobilization orders of the Battalion. From time to time these were looked at and kept up to date, but for many officers their details must have been unknown. In 1909 the Battalion took part in a practice mobilization, carried out as the real thing would be, except that men from other units took the place of the reservists. In 1912 the Battalion had found men in lieu of reservists for the practice mobilization of the Rifle Bde. In the winter of 1912/13 the Battalion had carried out a mobilization complete in every respect except that of personnel. That, when the actual order came in 1914, mobilization was completed within schedule time without a hitch, was a tribute to the care with which the orders had been compiled and showed that the lessons learnt from the practices had not gone unheeded.

The first sign of war came with a suddenness that would have surely found out the weakness in an ill-trained and undisciplined battalion.

On 29th July, 1914, the Battalion at Colchester was leading its normal life in a garrison town in England. No preparatory warning had been issued. The morning's work had given way to the usual round of cricket and tennis. The only officer in barracks was the orderly officer, and many of the men were " down town " when suddenly a telephone order came through that the " Precautionary Period " was to come into being. Under the orders for this the Battalion had to find one company at war strength for a composite battalion due to move to Felixstowe in two hours after receipt of the order. The order arrived at 4 p.m., and it is to the credit of those senior N.C.Os., who happened to be in barracks, and on whom the first brunt of the effort fell, that a company at full strength and equipped for war under Major Collins was shortly after on its march to the station. They remained at Felixstowe till 7th August, when their place was taken by troops of the Territorial Army.

The actual order to mobilize reached the Battalion between 6 and 7 p.m. on 4th August and, though handicapped by the absence of the Felixstowe detachment, was duly completed by midnight 8/9th August. The next few days were spent in field training and in hardening by route marches the reservists, now suddenly called back to the Colours from civilian life.

During this time Major Lambert superintended the construction of local defences in the vicinity of Colchester by troops of the Brigade.

For most of the officers it was a novelty to handle companies and platoons at war strength. Capt. Goodwyn and Lieut. Chadwicke were detailed for service with the New Armies, but Capt. Seabroke and Lieut. Hughes, on leave from foreign service, were sent to the Battalion, and Lieut. Richards, 2nd Lieuts. Salt, Wade and Hooper joined the Battalion from the Special Reserve. But even then the Battalion was one officer short of its war establishment.

On 18th August the Battalion entrained and moved to Harrow where the IVth Division was concentrated.

IVTH DIVISION.

G.O.C.   MAJOR GEN. SIR T. D'O. SNOW, C.B.,
consisting of
10th Infantry Bde.

11th Infantry Bde.

G.O.C.   BRIG. GEN. A. G. HUNTER WESTON, C.B., D.S.O.

1st Prince Albert's (Somerset Light Infantry).
1st The East Lancashire Regiment.
1st The Hampshire Regiment.
1st The Rifle Brigade (Prince Consort's Own).

12th Infantry Bde.

---

4 Brigades R.F.A., one heavy battery R.G.A.

2 Field companies R.E., and medical, cyclist, signal, A.S.C. units, divisional cavalry (one squadron) and ammunition column.

The Battalion remained at Harrow till the 21st August, when it was suddenly ordered to entrain for Southampton. So hurried was the move that some hundred and fifty men out on pass in the town had to be left behind and were brought on by the next battalion, joining their own battalion at Havre.

At dawn the Battalion embarked on the Braemar Castle 22nd Aug. on which were also Brigade Headquarters, the Somersets and a half battalion of the Hampshires. The ship sailed about 7.30 a.m., and, as far as the troops were concerned, for an unknown destination, and after an uneventful voyage arrived at Havre about 4 p.m. The Battalion, except the transport, had disembarked by 11 p.m., and then marched about four miles to a camp on the high ground above the town.

OFFICERS OF THE BATTALION ON LANDING IN FRANCE.

Lieut.-Col.	L. St. G. Le Marchant, D.S.O.	Commanding Officer
Major	T. S. Lambert	2nd in command
Major	E. R. Collins, D.S.O.	C company
Major	J. E. Green	D „
Capt.	G. T. Seabroke	D „
Capt.	E. E. Coventry	B „
Capt.	G. Clayhills, D.S.O.	A „
Capt.	A. St. L. Goldie	B „
Lieut.	J. F. Dyer	Machine Guns
Lieut.	F. D. Hughes	D company
Lieut.	E. C. Hopkinson	C „
Lieut.	F. E. Belchier	Adjutant
Lieut.	W. E. Dowling	C company
Lieut.	E. M. B. Delmege	B „
Lieut.	N. A. Leeson	A „
Lieut.	H. T. MacMullen	Transport
Lieut.	H. W. Canton	A company
Lieut.	W. M. Chisholm	D „
Lieut.	C. E. M. Richards [S.R.]	D „
2nd Lieut.	W. R. Tosswill	A „
2nd Lieut.	T. H. Mathews	C „
2nd Lieut.	R. Y. Parker	B „
2nd Lieut.	W. A. Salt [S.R.]	C „
2nd Lieut.	G. H. T. Wade [S.R.]	B „
2nd Lieut.	K. Hooper [S.R.]	A „
Hon. Lieut.	R. Longstaff	Quartermaster
Lieut.	R. A. Flood [R.A.M.C.]	Medical Officer

The Battalion transport was unloaded and arrived in 23rd Aug. camp about noon. The day was spent in camp till late in the evening when, amid much enthusiasm, the Battalion marched through the crowded streets of the town to the railway station, and entrained about 11 p.m.—destination being unknown.

At Havre two French interpreters presented themselves for attachment to the Battalion. Palpably but lately called back to the Colours from civilian life, clothed in the traditional képi, long blue coat and red trousers and armed with rather antediluvian rifles and bayonets of prodigious length, they were a never-ending source of amazement to the men. The one stuck to the Battalion through thick and thin; the other soon found the trials of the British Infantry too exacting and quietly disappeared.

The train, however, did not actually start for a consider- 24th Aug. able time, and when it did, moved with that slowness peculiar to French troop trains. Amiens was reached about noon. While the train lay in the station at Amiens, Col. R. Wanless O'Gowan, a former commanding officer of the Battalion, visited some of the officers and gave them the first information that fighting had actually begun, which was soon after borne out by a train of French wounded (Colonial troops) passing through the station.

At 7.30 p.m. the Battalion detrained at Le Cateau. There was some delay before the Battalion marched to Briaste, as the unloading facilities for the Transport were limited. The Battalion was informed that they were to march past F.M. Sir John French, who was at that time in the town; but this did not take place. After a short march of some five miles north Briaste was reached and the Battalion billeted in the village shortly before 10 p.m.

On the way up to Briaste the Battalion heard the first news of the war situation. As given out to company commanders on the line of march by the adjutant, it was graphic, but not very informative. " Have you heard the news ?

There's the hell of a German Army marching round our flank."

Indeed, that evening even Divisional Headquarters knew little more of the situation, as the information and immediate orders given to Gen. Snow on detraining at Le Cateau had been very sketchy.

25th Aug. At 5 a.m. the Battalion marched towards Solemnes where a position was taken up on the high ground South of the town astride the Le Cateau-Solemnes road, the 11th Brigade being in touch with French territorial troops and the 10th Brigade on the left, in order to cover the retirement of the 2nd Corps.

By noon, fleeing civilians, transport and fighting troops of the 2nd Corps, 19th Brigade, and some French territorial infantry began to dribble through in an orderly but hetero-geneous stream to Le Cateau and continued to do so throughout the afternoon. The sight of the already weary and war-worn units as they marched through the position held by the Battalion was hardly an auspicious commencement for the campaign. As officers and men of the Battalion watched the motley crowd go by, few indeed can have imagined that what they saw that afternoon was a mere nothing compared to what they themselves would be twenty-four hours later.

As the afternoon wore on the shells of the German advanced guard (apparently the 8th Division) could be seen bursting to the north of the town on the high ground held by cavalry and the rear-guard of the IIIrd Division. About 5 p.m. the Battalion was withdrawn and concentrated on the Solemnes-Le Cateau road east of Briaste, and marching through Briaste halted in a quarry on the western outskirts of the village.

By this time most of the villages to the north could be seen ablaze from German shells. Beyond what it could see for itself, the only information the Battalion had as to the situation was that it was to march in a westerly direction and take up a defensive position which it was understood was already being entrenched by civilian labour.

About 10 p.m. the Battalion marched in brigade westwards to Beauvois *via* Viesly and Bethencourt. A steady drizzle, darkness, roads deep in mud from a thunderstorm late in the afternoon, and a conglomeration of transport in Viesly, combined to delay the march so that Beauvois was not reached until long after midnight.

After reaching Beauvois the column turned south to Fontaine-au-Pire, a village practically continuous with the former. At the junction of Beauvois and Fontaine-au-Pire the column by mischance took the first instead of the second road to the west, and so after about half a mile the leading Battalions, of which the East Lancashire was one, found themselves in the fields at the end of a lane some five hundred yards north of Fontaine-au-Pire cemetery. The Brigade commander, who had been at the head of the column, now realizing that the wrong road had been taken, ordered the Battalions to settle down in the fields and await daylight, after taking some rough precautions for local defence. The effect of this was that the Brigade settled down for the night on the forward slope of the position it was to occupy, instead of on the position itself, causing valuable time to be lost in occupying it on the day breaking.

During this day the Battalion 1st Line transport halted on the Solemnes-Le Cateau road east of Briaste till about 3.30 p.m. when Lieut. MacMullen was ordered to move into Briaste. On arriving at Briaste, the information he received from passing troops led him on his own initiative to move southwest to Bethencourt. Near that village he happened to meet Capt. D'Esterre, a former adjutant of the Battalion and then acting as A.D.C. to the G.O.C. IVth Division, who told him to go on to Beauvois. The transport eventually halted in the streets of Fontaine-au-Pire about 11 p.m. During the night Lieut. MacMullen got in touch with the Rifle Bde., part of which was also in the village. But he was unable to locate the whereabouts of his own battalion.

This flank march of the IVth Division was ordered with the intention of clearing for the 2nd Corps the Le Cateau-Caudry position which was to be held for the night and the retreat to be continued further at 7 a.m. the following morning. But the pressure of the German advance, the difficulty of re-organizing the exhausted British cavalry and 2nd Corps, and the delay caused by the march of General Sordet's French cavalry corps from East to West across the British line of march occupied much time, so that many units did not reach their allotted bivouacs until far into the night. For these reasons it appeared to General Smith Dorrien in the early hours of the morning of the 26th that it would be impossible to retreat without first striking a blow at the enemy. He therefore decided to hold his ground [the IVth Division coming under his orders], and so to fight what was to be the battle of Le Cateau.

During the night the IVth Divisional Field Artillery reached the vicinity of the village of Ligny, but, expecting to retire at dawn, did not occupy battle positions. Further, the heavy battery, ammunition column, field ambulances, engineers, signal company, cyclists, divisional cavalry and A.S.C. train had as yet not reached the battle area, a fact that seriously handicapped the IVth Division in the battle to come. The absence of these units, still on their way up to the battle area, was of course accounted for by the hurried move from Havre.

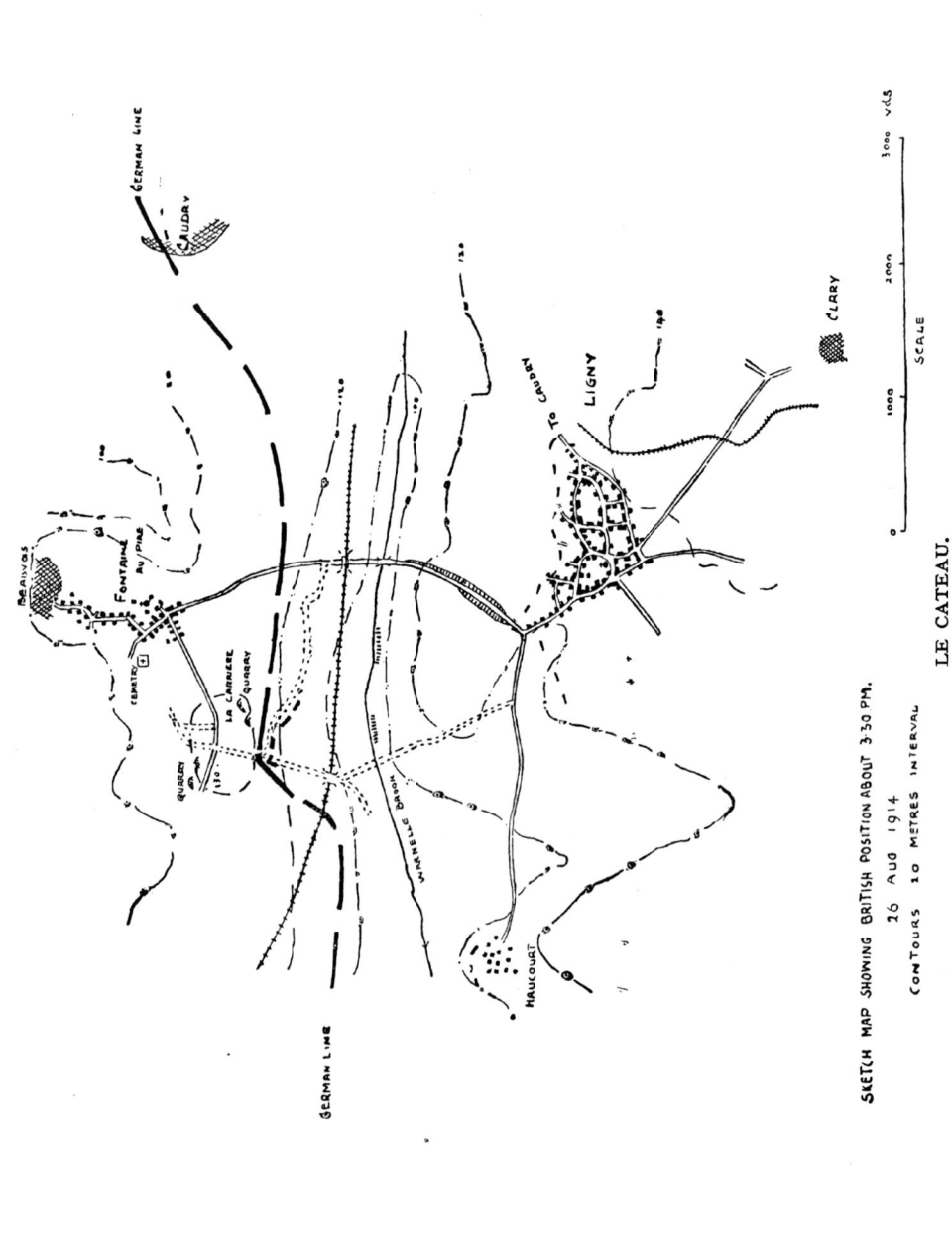

SKETCH MAP SHOWING BRITISH POSITION ABOUT 3·30 P.M.

26 AUG 1914

CONTOURS 10 METRES INTERVAL

LE CATEAU.

At dawn the Rifle Bde. and Somersets were moved north of Fontaine-au-Pire and into Beauvois and the Battalion remained on its bivouac ground. At the same time Lieut.-Col. Le Marchant and Major Lambert rode off to Beauvois, being ordered to report to divisional headquarters. Divisional H.Q. was, as a matter of fact, at Haucourt, but General Snow had himself been in Fontaine-au-Pire till late in the night. No explanation of this rather curious, though undoubted order can be traced.

In the absence of the commanding officer and 2nd in command, Major Collins, the next senior officer, rightly appreciating that there was danger to come, on his own initiative formed up the Battalion and moved it clear of the wire fences which, it so happened, enclosed the fields in which the Battalion had bivouacked, in order that it should be ready to move off directly the commanding officer returned. This timely anticipation of what was likely to be required may well have saved the Battalion from being caught by the enemy unprepared in mass formation on ground on which it would have been most difficult to deploy.

On the return of Lieut.-Col. Le Marchant the Battalion marched across country some thousand yards south to La Carriere, a flat ridge giving a good field of view and fire to the west and north west, but unsuitable for a defensive position to the north and north-east, the view being completely blocked by the villages of Beauvois and Fontaine-au-Pire in this direction, and there halted.

The 11th Brigade, by a divisional order of the previous evening issued at 5 p.m., had been ordered to occupy and entrench a position with La Carriere as its centre, but as it had only arrived at Fontaine-au-Pire in darkness there was considerable delay as to the exact disposition of the troops. The 10th and 12th Brigades of the IVth Division were on the left, but not in touch with the 11th, and as the divisional cavalry, cyclists and signal company were absent, local reconnaissance and transmission of orders was extremely difficult.

Meanwhile the IVth Division had at midnight received instructions from G.H.Q. that the retreat of the Division was to be continued in the early hours of the morning towards Peronne. The necessary orders to the Brigades were not however issued, as General Snow commanding the IVth Division, in the absence of his Signal Company had no means of rapid communication with his scattered troops except by mounted officers. At daybreak, therefore, the divisional commander was thinking of continuing the retreat as soon as the troops could be got on the move. Brig.-General Hunter Weston, the 11th Brigade Commander, who had received no information to this effect, on the other hand was thinking of occupying the La Carriere position to carry out the orders issued on the previous evening. Knowing nothing of the general situation the officers of the Battalion were merely thinking of an uncomfortable night in a muddy field, which had obviously been occupied lately by an army of cows. Since only small parties of hostile cavalry had as yet been seen, it was not realized by either the divisional, brigade or battalion commander that the German 19th Cavalry Brigade and three Jäger Battalions were rapidly closing on Beauvois.

About 5.30 a.m. General Snow received a request from General Smith Dorrien, commanding the 2nd Corps, to stand his ground and cover the left flank of the 2nd Corps. To this General Snow immediately agreed and despatched mounted officers to have his new orders carried into effect. It is curious to find that one of these, Capt. D'Esterre, was the first officer of the Regiment to be hit in the war.

However, this order reached the 11th Brigade too late to affect the situation as fighting had already begun. Though the Brigade, with the Hampshires on the left, the Rifle Bde. and East Lancashires in the centre, and the Somersets on the right, was approximately on the selected ground, the distribution of the troops on the ground had not been assigned, so that there was little cohesion between units, and each one eventually fought more or less where it found itself. Further, there was a gap between the right of the 11th Brigade and the left of the 7th Brigade (IIIrd Division) which was in position around Caudry. The divisional order issued at 5.30 a.m. directed this gap to be closed. It arrived too late.

About 5 a.m. rifle fire was heard in Beauvois village, as German cavalry (a brigade of the 9th Cavalry Division) attacked this village and Fontaine-au-Pire where the transport of the four Battalions still lay. Major Lambert was at this moment in Fontaine-au-Pire and was ordered by Gen. Hunter Weston to take command of the situation. He rapidly collected a force made up of the men of the transport, except the actual drivers, some men of the Rifle Bde., and the machine guns of the Battalion. Under cover of this force the Brigade transport, now formed into one unit under Lieut. MacMullen, hurriedly retired, led by a civilian guide, through Ligny to Caullery by order of the brigade major, the actual order being " go to Caullery and get to hell out of this." Major Lambert's force succeeded in repulsing the attack and then retired to the hollow south-east of La Carriere. In Major Lambert's official report of the action of the Battalion this day he refers to the " marked coolness in command of his party " of the Sgt. Master Cook, Sgt. Noden, who also accounted for some dozen Germans with his own rifle. This N.C.O. was imbued with a fine fighting spirit, as some time later he at his own request reverted to platoon sergeant in order that he might be in the line with his company commander, where he was killed not long after.

That the transport, through no fault of its own, was completely surprised is clear; that it was able to get away without loss was no doubt principally due to the capable handling of the situation by Major Lambert.

A divisional order issued at 5.30 a.m. directed Brig -Gen. Hunter Weston to move the transport clear of Fontaine-au-Pire and concentrate it by 8.30 a.m. in the valley between

Ligny and Fontaine-au-Pire. This message, of course, arrived after the fighting just recorded.

Lieut. MacMullen arrived at Caullery about 6.30 a.m. and halted there till about 1 p.m. During the morning he sent up part of the ammunition limbers to Ligny to form a reserve for the Brigade, some of these during the morning actually reaching the railway line immediately north of Ligny village.

The outbreak of rifle fire in Beauvois once again found the Battalion short of its two senior officers. Lieut.-Col. Le Marchant was at that moment riding round to inspect the ground and Major Lambert was, of course, at this time in Fontaine-au-Pire. The two next senior officers, Major Collins and Major Green, realizing that immediate action was necessary, therefore moved their own companies (C and D) north to hold the northern edge of La Carriere and commenced to dig in with their entrenching tools. A Company (Capt. Clayhills) and B Company (Capt. Coventry) remained on the road and a few minutes later were, on the return of the commanding officer, moved into the hollow south of La Carriere.

Soon after C Company (Major Collins) and D Company (Major Green) had got in position the front became rather congested with men, as a considerable number of Rifle Bde. and Somersets came into the same line. The left platoon of C Company also linked up with the Hampshires on its left.

An hour later found C Company under rifle, machine-gun and shrapnel fire, as the 3rd, 9th and 10th Jäger battalions reinforced the German Cavalry Brigade from Beauvois village. Casualties became frequent and A and B Companies were moved up closer to the support of C Company, which was now more or less in line with the Rifle Bde. and Somersets which had withdrawn from their advanced positions. Not long after this it became evident that trouble was to be expected on the left flank, as the left platoon of C Company (Lieut. Hopkinson) which was facing west, was engaged at about a thousand yards range with dismounted cavalry advancing towards Haucourt.

From German accounts this was the left of the 2nd German Cavalry Division advancing to attack the 12th British Infantry Brigade.

It is of interest to record that about this time Lieut. Hopkinson saw that relic of earlier warfare—a massed cavalry attack—take place north-west of Haucourt. German cavalry advanced at a deliberate pace some thousand to fifteen hundred strong in mass formation. The British line could not be seen. Suddenly there was a terrific outburst of rifle fire on which the mass instantaneously collapsed, absolutely shattered. It is but just to record that as they disappeared from view the survivors were still riding forward, and no man was seen to turn back. War it may not have been, but magnificent it certainly was. It was indeed a convincing demonstration of the maxim, so frequently instilled into the troops in their pre-war training, that infantry unless surprised had nothing to fear from massed cavalry.

Meanwhile Lieut.-Col. Le Marchant, anxious about his left flank, about 6.30 a.m. had ordered *D* Company (Major Green) to Haucourt, a village about a mile and a half to his left rear. Major Green on reaching Haucourt found it held by troops of the 10th and 12th Brigades and so returned to battalion headquarters near the bridge where the Fontaine-au-Pire–Ligny road crosses the railway south-east of La Carriere arriving shortly before 9 a.m. This incident clearly shows the lack of co-ordination between units, resulting from the universal ignorance of the situation. A single company was sent off to hold Haucourt, whereas in reality two brigades of infantry were grouped round that village.

In spite of a stout resistance, the German attack progressed, and by 10 a.m. *C* Company (Major Collins) was forced to retire by platoons about six hundred yards to the position occupied by *A* (Capt. Clayhills) and *B* (Capt. Coventry) Companies just north of the railway line between Fontaine-au-Pire and Ligny. It was in this retirement that Major Collins was wounded. Major Lambert in his official report of the

battle placed on record the " exceptional bravery and power
of command shown by this officer in withdrawing his company
from its difficult position." He had been the last man to leave
the advanced position. One young N.C.O., L/Cpl. Slater, the
son of an old Colour Sergeant of the Regiment, displayed
marked courage and determination, for when sent by Major
Collins with a message to Brig.-Gen. Hunter Weston he was
wounded ; and not only did he deliver the message, but set out
again to report to Major Collins that he had done so. Unfortunately he was shot in both legs before reaching Major
Collins and was eventually taken prisoner. Lieut. Hopkinson's
platoon of C Company received a verbal message to the effect
that Major Collins was retiring, but took this to be only information and not an order to retire, and so remained on the western
side of La Carriere with a company of the Rifle Bde. Lieut.
Salt and some twenty-five more men of C Company joined him.

In this position the Battalion remained throughout the
morning in spite of heavy shelling from the artillery of the
German 7th Reserve Division, which had been pushed on
rapidly ahead of its infantry to support the cavalry and
Jäger attack.

The line held by the Brigade was now approximately
as follows from left to right :—

Hampshires in the low ground near the railway south-
west of La Carriere.

Lieut. Hopkinson's platoon of C Company [E. Lan. R.]
at the south-western corner of La Carriere.

Rifle Bde. along the southern edge of La Carriere.

Part of the Somersets continuing the line eastwards.

East Lancashires in close support just north of the railway
line behind the Rifle Bde.

The German attack now died away for a time. Opposite
the 11th Brigade it had made little progress.

Soon after noon the position on the left flank became
serious, as the Hampshires were being pressed back from the
railway line eight hundred yards south-west of La Carriere,

and, as Germans could be seen in the scrub near the railway line, Major Green was ordered to send two platoons of *D* Company under Lieuts. Chisholm and Richards to clear up this area, and to assist the Hampshires to stabilize the left flank. This was effected for the time being.

About 12.30 p.m. the Battalion came under enfilade fire from machine guns from the east and suffered considerable loss. The pressure on this flank was due to the loss of Caudry, the village held by the 7th Brigade some two miles east of La Carriere. It was as a matter of fact partly retaken by the British some three hours later.

Soon after 2 p.m. the infantry of the German 7th Reserve Division reached the scene of battle, and the pressure became so great not only on the front but on both flanks that General Hunter Weston, after hearing the opinion of Lieut.-Col. Le Marchant and the commanding officer of the Hampshires, decided to withdraw the Brigade to Ligny village immediately, as he had been previously ordered to do when it became necessary.

Ligny village lies on the high ground some fourteen hundred yards in the rear across a broad valley devoid for the most part of any cover, and in full view of the enemy's artillery observers and their advanced machine guns.

Lieut. Hopkinson's party, the company of the Rifle Bde. and a small party of Somersets were ordered by General Hunter Weston, personally, to hold on to the sunken road along the southern edge of La Carriere to cover this retirement.

The Brigade, less most of the Hampshires, who shortly before retired rather to the west of Ligny and two companies of the Somersets, who had earlier been withdrawn to Ligny, was formed up in the dead ground of the Warnelle brook to the south-east of La Carriere under the personal command of General Hunter Weston in close order, but, owing to the difficulty of concentrating the scattered companies, units were considerably entangled and the frontage was very narrow. The actual order for the retirement was given verbally to the assembled troops by the brigade commander, and in this difficult position was misunderstood, so that the Brigade moved off together practically in mass, contrary to the intention of the brigade commander.

The approach of the Brigade into the open in this dense formation, as it commenced to climb the long slope towards Ligny, totally devoid of cover, was the signal for a perfect inferno of shrapnel and machine-gun fire from the Germans, causing considerable loss. Companies and platoons became hopelessly disorganized in spite of the efforts of officers and of General Hunter Weston himself, who, on having his horse shot under him, undauntedly remarked as he looked at it, " What a glorious death. Bring me my second horse." Throughout the morning he had shown a conspicuous disregard for the heaviest fire in personally visiting and encouraging the men in the firing line, though perhaps his capable Brigade Major at Brigade H.Q. thereby found his work the more arduous. The majority of the casualties were caused by machine-gun fire, as, although the shell fire was very heavy, most of the shrapnel burst too high. It was indeed fortunate that the German shrapnel fire was inefficient, as few reached Ligny without being bruised by the gunfire.

It was only during the latter part of the retirement that the Brigade had any covering fire from the British guns on Ligny ridge, as, through lack of co-operation between infantry and artillery, and until the artillery could see for themselves, they were unaware of what was taking place.

At the same time the rear party still left on the sunken road at La Carriere were heavily attacked but held their ground.

On reaching Ligny the Battalion was very disorganized, as companies and platoons had in the retirement become inextricably entangled. However, officers collected the nearest men round them and, in conjunction with the Rifle Bde. and Somersets, the defence of the village was organized.

It is impossible to unravel the details of the defence of

Ligny. The Battalion was mainly in two parts. Near the north-western corner were Lieut.-Col. Le Marchant, Major Green, and Captain Clayhills, but the greater part of the Battalion were at the north-eastern corner under Major Lambert, Capt. Coventry, and Capt. Seabroke. Capt. Seabroke on reaching the extreme right, found a considerable number of the Somersets and, as there was no senior officer of that Regiment present, took command of them temporarily. Some time later Major Green moved over from the western to the eastern part of the village. The entrances of the village were barricaded and field guns were brought into the village for close action. At the east end of the village Major Lambert found a machine gun of the 6th Dragoon Guards which assisted the defence in this quarter.

Nor was this any too soon as, shortly before 4 p.m., large German forces broke through between La Carriere and Caudry and advanced south towards Ligny, while the German guns shelled this village. However, this advance presented a magnificent target for the British guns grouped around Ligny and, with the assistance of rifle fire from the infantry holding the east end of the village, the advance was brought to a complete standstill with severe losses before it reached the Warnelle brook.

In the meanwhile the rear party, now completely isolated on the sunken road at La Carriere, was being more and more hard pressed. The pressure was greatest on the left flank which was held by the East Lancashire party. Casualties were so heavy that this flank could not have been held but for the Rifle Bde., which frequently gave them the most unstinted and gallant assistance in spite of its own troubles. About 3 p.m., after much difficulty, improvised signalling communication with Ligny was obtained, only to find that no help could be expected from that quarter. The senior sub-altern of the Rifle Bde. and Lieut. Hopkinson therefore decided to hold on till dusk, as a retirement across the open valley in daylight seemed impossible.

In this defence Corporal Lismore, in spite of the fact that the range-finder and then his rifle had been smashed in his hands earlier in the day, stood out by his courage and determination in a fight where all did well, even the wounded pluckily assisting the defence by crawling up and down the line distributing ammunition. Sgt. Hughes, the platoon sergeant, also did excellent work, and later on in the war received a commission. Pte. Beaumont showed a marked power of command that two months later brought him promotion to sergeant, unhappily soon after which he was killed.

However, by 5 p.m. their ammunition was all but exhausted, and the Germans had not only advanced to within a hundred yards of the sunken road, but both flanks, shot into at the same range, were being steadily encircled. After firing off the last of their ammunition in one final burst of rapid fire the whistle went and the survivors, now a mere handful of men and four subalterns, two of whom were wounded, bolted, every man for himself, to the cover at the bottom of the valley, reformed there and retired on Ligny, but with happier results than those which had attended the retirement of the Battalion three hours earlier.

As the German infantry rushed on to the southern face of La Carriere, the British Field Artillery to the west of Ligny village opened fire with such effect that the German advance was not only brought to a complete standstill, but no further advance from that direction was attempted again that day. The shooting of the British Artillery was magnificent, the shrapnel ploughing great lanes through the dense German masses at about two thousand yards range and causing very heavy losses.

Had it not been for this artillery support it must have fared ill with the rear party, as, so impossible had it been to disentangle the units now defending Ligny, the only rifle covering fire for this party, as they climbed the exposed slope to Ligny, was a group of twelve officers, General Hunter Weston, his Brigade Major, the commanding officers of the

East Lancashires and the Rifle Bde., their two adjutants, Captain Clayhills, Lieuts. Delmege and Canton, three subalterns of the Rifle Bde., and less than half a dozen men of the two regiments.

For three hours the company of the Rifle Bde. and East Lancashire party—perhaps two hundred and eighty men all told—had held up the full weight of the German attack. Less than seventy survivors can have reached Ligny.

The last burst of rapid fire before retiring from the sunken road gave the party perhaps one hundred yards start before the Germans realized what was happening, but the last two hundred yards to the railway embankment were covered under a hail of machine-gun and rifle bullets from both flanks. From the cover at the bottom of the valley up to Ligny the party came under little fire and suffered few casualties as, being widely extended, it presented but a poor target for those Germans who faced the fire of the British guns. It is to the credit of the men of both Regiments that after the ' sauve qui peut ' to the railway the officers had no difficulty in reforming and extending the men.

For the defence of the sunken road Corporal Lismore was mentioned in despatches and received the Medaille Militaire, being selected by his commanding officer as the N.C.O. of the Battalion the most deserving to receive the one French decoration given to N.C.Os. and men of the Battalion for the Retreat. This N.C.O. was possessed of an iron nerve given to few, as before leaving the sunken road a badly wounded man, conscious but in awful agony, begged him to shoot him. Corporal Lismore, after obtaining permission from his officer, put his rifle to the man's head and fired.

For holding on to this position Lieut. Hopkinson subsequently received the Military Cross and was mentioned in despatches.

About 6.30 p.m. there was a threat of a second attack on Ligny village from the East, but this did not materialize. Although there was no actual attack, German troops reached the area of Montigny-Bertry soon after dusk where before dawn they cut off a detachment of the IIIrd Division, principally Gordons.   It appears to be this German force which was seen from Ligny moving round the right flank of that village.

Late in the afternoon Brig.-Gen. Hunter Weston was ordered to retire, and soon afterwards it was decided to evacuate the village.   The time was propitious as the German attack had died away, and there was no pressure on the defenders of the village.

As there was no Transport all the wounded who could not walk were collected in the church and had to be left behind. The Battalion medical officer, Lieut. Flood, R.A.M.C., with the customary self-sacrifice of his Corps, decided that his first duty was to the wounded, and so stayed with them. Major Lambert in his official report refers to the excellent work done by this officer earlier in the day in the firing line in spite of the scanty means at his disposal, as the maltese cart on which were the stretchers, had retired with the transport, so that the action was fought without any medical equipment.

The Battalion retired from Ligny village in four parties, all companies being still hopelessly mixed up, and it was merely a case of each officer taking out such men as he could collect, often also those of other battalions, around him.

Major Lambert withdrew his troops some two hundred and fifty strong (mainly *B* Company) along the railway line from the east of Ligny village to Clary.   When half-way to Clary he ordered *B* Company (Capt. Coventry) to take up a position on the ridge between the two villages to cover the retirement.   This company withdrew to Clary shortly after. One officer and a detachment of about seventy men struck south westerly towards Malincourt where eventually they joined Major Green.   It is unknown who this officer was.

Major Green, who was about to move off in conjunction with Major Lambert, was, however, personally ordered by Col. Edmonds, G.S.O.I., IVth Division, to make south-west for the high ground near Selvigny, where he was informed the divisional commander was forming an infantry rearguard. Major Green took out four officers and some two hundred and eighty men, of whom perhaps two hundred were East Lanca-shires, after taking steps to inform Major Lambert of his fresh orders. This information never reached Major Lambert, and Major Green's force did not rejoin the Battalion for four days. That it had survived was not even known for some days. Prior to this Lt.-Col. Le Marchant had sent an order to Major Green directing him to retire to Clary, but this message never reached Major Green.

Finally, rather before 7 p.m. Lt.-Col. Le Marchant went round the village and collected such officers and men of the Battalion as were still left behind. This little party, consisting of Lt.-Col. Le Marchant, Captains Seabroke, Clayhills and Goldie, and Lieuts. Hopkinson, Belchier, Richards, Salt and Wade, with perhaps 50 other ranks, disconsolately wandered out of the village near the south-western corner and, striking south, reached the railway line to Clary near which place it was joined by Major Lambert's and Capt. Coventry's parties. On reaching Clary the village was to be found occupied by a considerable number of stragglers of the III., IV., and Vth Divisions, and Brig.-Gen. Hunter Weston, taking command, set off at the head of the dejected and unordered column for Malincourt.

The Brigade retired from Ligny in six main parties and many smaller ones. Although some of these united by the 28th August, the Brigade was not finally concentrated as one unit till 30th August.

We last left the Brigade transport at Caullery. Soon after noon a considerable number of wounded men of the 12th Brigade drifted through Caullery, and about 2 p.m. a staff officer of the IVth Division rode by and told Lieut. MacMullen to go to Malincourt *via* Walincourt. Lieut. MacMullen there-fore moved the transport across country south of Selvigny towards Walincourt. Near this village a message was received that the transport of the Rifle Bde. was needed at Elincourt.

c

Lieut. MacMullen thinking—and rightly so—that if the Rifle Bde. transport was wanted to go to Elincourt, it was probable that the remainder of the Brigade would be near by, therefore took all the transport to Elincourt, arriving about 3 p.m. He waited there for some time, and then finding no sign of the fighting troops of the Brigade decided to make for Malincourt, in accordance with his previous orders, utilizing such few spare men as he had to form his own advanced guard.

However, when about one mile short of Malincourt he was met by a gunner officer who said it was useless to go to Malincourt, and suggested a retirement to Serain. This course was adopted, and Serain was reached about 5.30 p.m. While in this village a staff officer rode by and ordered the transport to St. Quentin, remarking that the troops had had the hell of a day, but were retiring in perfect order !

The transport moved off down the Estrees road to reach the main Cambrai–St. Quentin road, but almost immediately there was an alarm of an attack, and a defensive position was taken up with all available men.   This alarm, however, proved unfounded, and the march continued in the midst of a stream of transport moving south-west from Le Cateau.   About 6.30 p.m. a staff officer of the IVth Division passed by in a motor car, giving a most doleful account of the day, but no orders as to what was to be done.   All evening long the disorganized stream of transport and troops moved down towards the Cambrai–St. Quentin road, and at dusk Lieut. MacMullen halted by the roadside near Nauroy on his own initiative.

To return to the Battalion ; the order to retire from Ligny had given Malincourt as a point of concentration for the IVth Division, but on reaching Elincourt at 11 p.m. the column, now made up of considerably less than half of the survivors of the 11th Brigade and many stragglers, found the roads blocked by masses of weary soldiery of the IIIrd Division, and as it was also rumoured that the Germans had reached Malincourt, settled down in the streets for the night.   A little food was obtained for the men of the Battalion from the villagers, and the northern entrance was barricaded on which a guard was placed.

As Lieut.-Col. Le Marchant's party cleared Ligny they saw the gun teams galloping up to save the guns which, though quite unsupported by any organized infantry, were still in position to the left of the village. The shattered infantry may gratefully remember the devotion of the artillery which, heedless of their own safety, remained in the line to the bitter end of a sorry day.

During the march to Clary considerable gun-fire was heard to the far west. It was Gen. Sordet's French cavalry corps coming into action to take the strain off the British. It was a heartening sound, as in some curious and unknown way the troops in Ligny had heard that they might expect help from the French on their left flank during the day.

On this day the Battalion lost Major Collins, wounded and taken prisoner; Lieut. Chisholm—a promising young officer—who died of wounds in Ligny the following day and is buried in Ligny cemetery; 2nd Lieut. Salt wounded; 2nd Lieut. Hooper, wounded and taken prisoner (who later in the war made a gallant but ineffective effort to escape from Germany); Lieut. Flood, R.A.M.C., taken prisoner, and two hundred and fifty-seven other ranks, killed, wounded and missing, of whom a hundred and thirty belonged to C Company. It is unknown how many of the casualties were actually killed or taken prisoner, but it can safely be said that no unwounded man of the Battalion was taken prisoner. Lieut.-Col. Le Marchant was slightly wounded in his foot, but, though lame, retained command of the Battalion till his death on 9th September. In the brigade commander's report on the battle he refers to Lieut.-Col. Le Marchant as "a capable battalion commander and gallant man."

The Battalion also lost all its drums at Ligny. How this actually happened is unknown. They were probably just thrown away as the drummers had as much and more than they could do in the fight without being encumbered by a drum.

Part of the Battalion War Memorial is a set of silver drums and bugles on which are inscribed the names of the battles in which the Battalion took part in the Great War.

The casualties of the 11th Brigade were about thirty officers and eleven hundred other ranks, killed, wounded and missing.

No record of the German losses opposite the 11th Brigade can yet be found. They must have been very heavy as they greatly outnumbered the British, and the attack, pressed at times with the greatest vigour and supported by a far heavier weight of artillery than the British could bring to bear, had only made one to two miles of ground. Moreover, they were too exhausted for an immediate pursuit, for the 7th German Reserve Division, halting for the night on the line Haucourt–La Carriere, did not receive its orders to continue the advance till the early hours of the morning of the 27th August.

In fact, so stubborn had been the defence of the La Carriere–Ligny positions that the Germans, though passing south on both sides of it, did not enter Ligny till well on into the next day, and a small party of stragglers of the IVth Division, who found themselves in Ligny on the morning of the 27th, actually escaped north-west out of the village and reached the Channel Ports.

An appreciative comment on the stubborn fight put up by the British Army this day appears in the memoirs of Von Kluck's chief of staff : " One cannot refuse to recognize the bold attitude of the British troops who succeeded, even at the price of heavy losses, in carrying out their withdrawal in the middle of the fight."

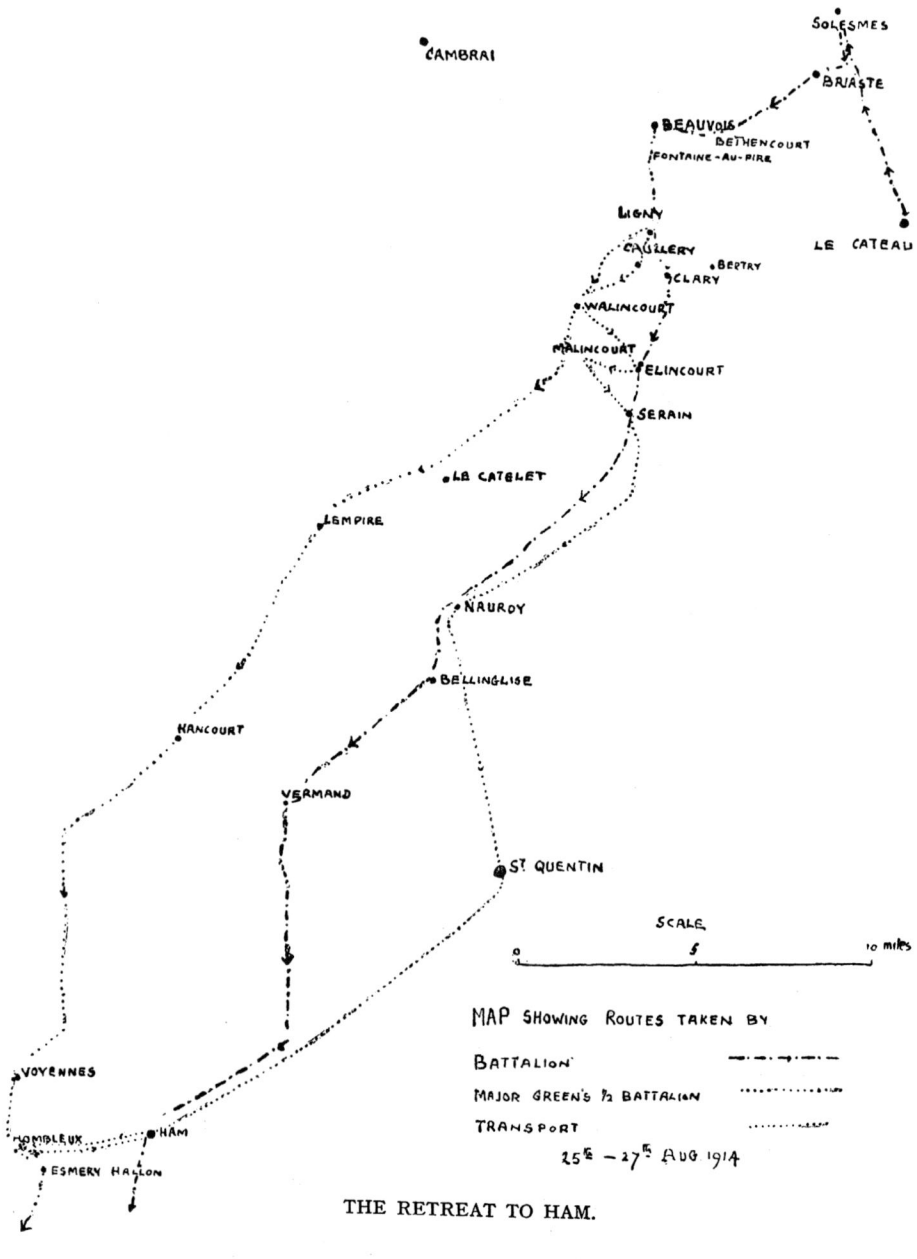

CAMBRAI

SOLESMES

BRIASTE

BEAUVOIS
BETHENCOURT
FONTAINE-AU-PIRE

LE CATEAU

LIGNY

CAULLERY

BERTRY

CLARY

WALINCOURT

MALINCOURT

FELINCOURT

SERAIN

LE CATELET

LEMPIRE

NAUROY

BELLINGLISE

HANCOURT

VERMAND

St QUENTIN

VOYENNES

HOMBLEUX

HAM

ESMERY HALLON

SCALE

0   5   10 miles

MAP SHOWING ROUTES TAKEN BY

BATTALION

MAJOR GREEN'S ½ BATTALION

TRANSPORT

25th – 27th AUG 1914

THE RETREAT TO HAM.

But there was to be little rest. At 2 a.m. the Brigade 27th Aug. was ordered to fall in, and for the first time since Ligny the men fell in by their right companies, and a line of march was formed with the battalions in regular order. The Battalion was the rear-guard to the column and C Company the rear party. This company was now reduced to Lieut. Hopkinson and twenty-five men (the other survivors being with Major Green), but he increased his command by half a dozen mounted men, all of different regiments, and so moved off. As the Battalion left Elincourt memories of 1870 were vividly brought to mind, as the inhabitants could be seen opening the graves in the cemetery in which they were hiding their valuables.

As the column, led by a civilian guide, moved off in the darkness it was joined by numerous stragglers from other units, but even then was probably only some thousand strong, as many parties had not rejoined the Brigade after the retirement from the Ligny position.

After reaching Serain where the Brigade Major joined with a considerable party which he had brought out of Ligny, the Brigade, to avoid the congested roads, struck across the open country for Nauroy, which was reached about 9.30 a.m., and there halted, food being obtained from the willing villagers.

It was intended to make a halt at Nauroy for three hours, but the German pursuit was closing quicker than the British knew, and the tired and hungry troops did not even have time to finish their meal, as about 11 a.m. shells fell on the village from the advanced guard of German cavalry and cyclists, supported by light artillery, at a thousand yards range. The outposts found by the Irish Horse were driven in, and the Hampshires were ordered to engage the enemy in order to cover the retirement of the remainder of the Brigade.

In this withdrawal, unfortunately, the Brigade became yet more separated, for one half under Capt. Boyd, the brigade major, lost touch with Brig.-Gen. Hunter Weston and took a westerly direction. This party, consisting of the major part of the Somersets, Hampshires and Rifle Bde., marched to Tertry, where late in the afternoon it happened to find a column of the IVth Division with artillery, which assisted the men by giving them a lift on the limbers. This column then marched to Voyennes, which it reached early on the morning of the 28th, and joined the most western column of the 11th Brigade under Lieut.-Col. Biddulph, with whom was Major Green, with nearly half of the Battalion.

Capt. Seabroke, when the firing broke out at Nauroy, had, while his men put on their equipment, gone off down the village street to see what was happening, and on returning found no trace of the Battalion. However, seeing the Hampshires in the open country near by, he joined them and remained with them till Voyennes.

The Battalion itself withdrew in extended order to the Cambrai–St. Quentin Canal, about a thousand yards west of Nauroy. Shells fell around the Battalion but no man was actually hit. On reaching the Canal, which was in a deep and heavily wooded ravine, the Battalion reformed. The Brigade, now reduced to Brig.-Gen. Hunter Weston, the East Lancashires about four hundred strong, and some two hundred men of other battalions, was then led by the Brigade Commander personally in column of route to Bellinglise. Under cover of hedges and woods they succeeded in skilfully avoiding a considerable force of German cavalry, which were only about a thousand yards to the right flank of the column, and which, although at one time in a most favourable position to cut off the Brigade, never discovered it.

The weary march, the little force being quite isolated, was then continued to Vermand, where a piece of dry bread for each man was obtained from the villagers, and then by Fluquries to Ham. Nearly one hundred years earlier the

Regiment had marched through Vermand (also on the way to Paris, but after Waterloo). This march was very slow and tiring, as frequent halts had to be made to explore the country in order to avoid further attentions from the German cavalry, who were suspected to be hanging round us. The latter part of the march was unmolested by the enemy. In fact, the German cavalry, held up by parties of stragglers, had halted not far south of Bellinglise for the night. Ham, crowded by transport and troops of the 2nd Corps, was eventually reached about 7 p.m., and the Battalion was finally billeted in a timber-yard, but little food could be obtained for the men.

During the seventeen hours' march the Battalion, without proper halts, little food, and worried by the enemy, had covered over thirty miles under most trying conditions, and when it is remembered that for the previous thirty-six hours it had been continually marching or fighting, and had had only four hours' sleep during a period of sixty-three hours, it well earned the praise of its Brigade Commander, General Hunter Weston : " I have a high regard for the 1st East Lancs. That grand march of theirs to Ham, their cheeriness in whistling and singing after the heavy day's fighting and that thirty-five mile march, their determination and splendid spirit in marching back two and a half miles after no rest and very little food to take up night outposts, will ever remain in my memory as one of the finest episodes of the war."

Lieut. MacMullen with the 1st line transport left his bivouac near Nauroy about 7 a.m. and set off for St. Quentin in the midst of a disorganized crowd of soldiery. Soon after he was joined by a subaltern and small party of the Somersets who had lost their way after Ligny, and who now took over escort to the brigade transport, which escort was later in-creased by a small detachment of the K.O.Y.L.I. (Vth Division).

St. Quentin was reached about 11 a.m. At St. Quentin a staff officer was seen holding up a large board on which was written " IVth Division to Ham," and directions for other

divisions.   An army chaplain was also doing useful work by
issuing rolls of bread to the men as they passed by.   After
clearing St. Quentin the transport halted two hours, and Lieut.
MacMullen succeeded in buying food from a villager for the
men.   It is curious to relate that the old lady in question
refused English gold and demanded francs.   She would hardly
have done so later !

Ham was reached about 5 p.m., and, seeing the staff of the
2nd Corps in the Town Hall, Lieut. MacMullen asked for orders
and was told to collect all available men he could find and
take up a defensive position to cover Ham.   While doing this
the order was countermanded, as it was discovered that the
11th Brigade were still to the north of the town.   He was
then ordered to go on in a south-westerly direction to Hombleux.   This he did, and there halted, but rode back into Ham
again himself to obtain further information.   He there
happened to meet Major Lambert, and so found the Battalion
and brought the transport back to Ham.

28th Aug.   During the night Brig.-Gen. Hunter Weston had been
placed in command by Gen. Smith Dorrien of such troops in
Ham as could be collected for its defence, and at 3 a.m., as
it was again rumoured that the Germans were advancing from
the north-east, the Battalion was ordered to take up an outpost position some two miles north of the town where civilian
labour had been enlisted for digging trenches.   This rumour
was once more incorrect, as a large part of the IIIrd Division
and the 19th Brigade were still between Ham and the enemy.
The Battalion did not occupy these trenches and remained
by the roadside near the cemetery in the cold of the morning
while troops of the IIIrd Division and 19th Brigade passed
through.   At 6 a.m. the Battalion was ordered to continue the
retreat south, in conformance with the intention of G.H.Q.
that the 2nd Corps was to retire south of the Oise that day
under cover of the 1st and 2nd Cavalry Brigades, the IVth
Division, and a part of the IIIrd Division.   A halt was made

just south of the town for nearly two hours, when the Battalion moved on again.

About 6 a.m., Brig.-Gen. Hunter Weston rode over to Voyennes by himself where he had found out the main portion of his Brigade was now concentrated. He instructed Lieut.-Col. Le Marchant to march to Noyon direct, as both the Ham and Voyennes columns were to move towards Noyon that day.

As the day wore on the chill of the morning gave place to what was probably the hottest day of the year, and the twelve miles to Noyon seemed unending with the glaring sun, broken only by the tall poplars on either side of the straight and dusty French road. The march was slow and irregular, as units of the IIIrd, IVth and Vth Divisions and 19th Brigade moved fitfully along the crowded road. Companies even of different regiments were often two abreast, and at times a third line would yet be added of guns and transport crowded with men who could no longer walk. Of march discipline over and above companies there was little. Units halted and passed each other when and where they chose. To make confusion worse confounded, fleeing civilians with every imaginable conveyance from large farm carts to perambulators also used this Via Dolorosa. Latterly the disorder was yet further increased by the arrival of small patrols of French cavalry looking, amid the dusty and mud-covered khaki troops, curiously out of place in their black plumed helmets and gaily coloured uniforms of 1914. The heat of the day was excessive and the irregular march in clouds of dust was a severe ordeal for the troops. Water at the roadside was tempting, and on one occasion had to be issued under a guard with fixed bayonets. That no man of the Battalion broke the ranks or fell out until he collapsed entirely will remain for ever as an honourable record.

Noyon was reached about 3 p.m., and as the column neared the town it straightened itself out, staff officers making great and successful efforts to reduce chaos into order. The Battalion was directed into bivouac in the grounds of the chateau half a mile south of Sempigny, a village some three miles south of the Oise River.   Bivouac was reached about 5 p.m.   Half rations were issued that night by the A.S.C.   This was the first proper meal the Battalion had for seventy-two hours.

The strength of the Battalion that night was under four hundred, all ranks, Major Green's half Battalion being still away.

The transport this day left Ham about 2 a.m. and marched to Noyon, arriving about noon.   It was there ordered to go on to Bailly (some five miles south of Sempigny) and await the arrival of the Battalion.   This it did, and there halted for the night, being quite unaware of the whereabouts of the Battalion.   A G.H.Q. order had ordered all officers' kits and even military material to be burnt on the roadside, but luckily this order never reached Lieut. MacMullen, and so the Battalion escaped this additional hardship.

With reference to the period 27th August to 29th August, Brig.-Gen. Hunter Weston a short while afterwards sent in the following report to his divisional commander :

" I have the honour to bring to your notice the action of the 1st Bn. East Lancashire Regiment, [he then briefly narrates the story of the three days.]   This instance of endurance, cheeriness and fine military spirit is the more worthy of record when it is remembered that these men had been marching and fighting without omission since Le Cateau.   The principal credit for this meritorious performance is due amongst the officers to :

Lieut.-Col. Le Marchant, ' whose example of cheeriness and self-possession, and whose handling of his men was beyond praise.'

Lieut. A/Adj. Belchier, ' who was indefatigable in keeping the men together and making arrangements for such food and rest as it was possible to get them.'
And amongst the N.C.Os. :

C.S.M. Burgess and Sgt. Pattinson ' for gallantry and
coolness when the column was shelled at Nauroy,
and by their example did much to keep the men
together. They were invaluable in controlling and
encouraging the tired men.' "

About noon the transport rejoined the Battalion and the 29th Aug.
welcome rest was not broken till late in the afternoon when
the Battalion (except Lieut. Dyer's machine-gun detachment,
which moved north again to the Oise River to cover the
preparations for the demolition of the bridges), marched by a
rough track to a new bivouac at Les Cloyes two miles north-
west of Carlepont. Shortly before moving off the transport
of the western 11th Brigade column came in—a curious collec-
tion of farm carts filled with the wounded and weary, and in
some cases drawn by three yoke of oxen. These proved an
endless source of worry to Lieut. MacMullen, as their pace was
so slow that they could only be kept in the column for the next
three days by missing the hourly halts.

The order to move was hurried and produced one of the
humorous incidents of war. Lieut. Belchier, the adjutant,
was caught by the order with one side of his face shaved and
a four-days' growth yet on the other side, and thus he remained
for two days.

The chateau at Sempigny is no more. Fighting later in
the war has left hardly a stone to mark its existence.

We must now follow the misfortunes of Major Green
and to what amounted to half of the Battalion. We left him
leaving Ligny on 26th August about 6 p.m., under orders to
go to Selvigny, where he expected to find his divisional commander organizing a rear-guard. On reaching Selvigny he
found no British troops at all, and, having no further orders,
he decided to retire south, and eventually reached Malincourt
about dusk, after an anxious march along the light railway
line. Malincourt, the rallying point of the IVth Division,
was one chaotic mass of infantry and artillery. Among these
were an officer of the Battalion and some fifty men. This
unexpected addition brought Major Green's command up to
three hundred and fifty men (of whom two hundred and eighty
were East Lancashires) with Lieuts. Dowling and Mathews of
C Company, Leeson and Canton of A Company, and Parker
of B Company. After a short halt Major Green marched on to
Lempire—a distance of fourteen miles from Ligny, arriving
about 2 a.m. This was the route followed by the main part
of the IVth Division, Lieut.-Col. Biddulph of the Rifle Bde.
assuming command of this part of the 11th Brigade, some
twelve hundred men, principally Somersets, East Lancashires
and Rifle Bde.

27th Aug.   At 5 a.m. the march was continued to Hancourt with a
two-hour halt at Hervilly on the way. Hancourt was reached
about noon, and in conjunction with the 10th and 12th Brigades
the column took up a defensive position to cover the retirement
of the 2nd Corps to the Somme, where Gen. Joffre had requested
the British to hold their ground while large French reinforce-
ments were brought up on the left flank.

The afternoon was spent by Major Green in digging

trenches, in the course of which a French General officer came to see Major Green, but co-operation between the two armies, owing to the French General's limited English and Major Green's limited French, did not get much beyond the French General gravely saluting the British Army and Major Green's returning the compliment—actions which no doubt advanced the harmony of the two allied nations, but could do little towards solving the immediate tactical problems.

During the afternoon the British Cavalry were in touch with the German advanced troops some four miles to the north of Hancourt and the French force, consisting of Gen. Sordet's cavalry corps and the 61st and 62nd Reserve Divisions, were in action some six miles to the west.

However, German infantry did not reach Lempire till late in the afternoon, and the IVth Division was withdrawn without becoming engaged.

The exhaustion of the troops that evening was so great that country carts, sometimes drawn by oxen, had to be requisitioned for the weary infantry. Infantry were also placed on the limbers of the artillery, the 29th battery R.F.A. assisting Major Green's half Battalion. A system was devised whereby each infantry man in turn should get an hour's ride with the artillery, but as the column marched pitifully on through the night this broke down, and at times even the guns themselves could hardly be seen for the infantry men lying prostrate and haphazardly on them. So unwonted and tragic was the sight that it caused an infantry officer, as he looked on the remnants of his command, half meaningly to mutter the doleful reflection, " What a —— rabble ! "—a remark to which a certain senior officer, who happened to be riding by, took great exception, expressing himself in no uncertain terms, only to be countered by the reply, " Well, just look at them for yourself, Sir. Aren't they ? " Chaotic as the column may have been that night, discipline told, and all that was needed was a few hours' rest to turn it once more into an effective fighting force.

28th Aug. Voyennes was reached about 5.30 a.m. and food was obtained from the kindly villagers for the men. Here Capt. Seabroke and a few men joined Major Green. By now the two columns of the 11th Brigade were only four miles apart, and Brig.-Gen. Hunter Weston moved over from the eastern to the western column. Major Green thus heard for the first time of the survival of the other half Battalion after Ligny. About 10 a.m. the retreat was continued *via* Hombleux to Esmery Hallon, with the 11th Brigade as rear-guard to the Division, where a halt was made till 7 p.m. Then they started once again, Major Green's half Battalion being the rear party, to Freniche, where the troops lay down by the roadside for the night in the Bois de l'Hôpital under cover of outposts found by the Battalion.

Soon after arrival at Freniche there was an alarm of an attack on the outpost line. In the failing light the observation line, seeing a cloud of dust coming down the road, rapidly retired on the picquet line. Dispositions were made for a resolute defence against what was reported to be a considerable force of the enemy. However, things are not always as they seem, for the cloud of dust turned out to be but a flock of sheep being driven down the road by a leisurely Frenchman.

29th Aug. At 4 a.m. Major Green continued the march *via* Campagne to Sermaize which was reached at 8 a.m.

This was the day of the withdrawal and concentration of the 2nd Corps and IVth Division south of the Oise.

To cover this the 11th Brigade took up a position near Sermaize which it held throughout the day. As the afternoon passed the situation of the Brigade became extremely critical. German cavalry had been seen passing round their left flank, and were also advancing south from Ham. This Brigade, now practically the only British force north of the River, was therefore in immediate danger of being cut off.

So serious did the position appear that the divisional commander entertained but little hope of being able to extricate the Brigade from its dangerous position. Brig.-Gen. Hunter Weston fixed a rendezvous south of the river near Sempigny in case the units became separated, and pointed out that if the worst happened there were yet two alternatives, viz., to make the best of their way to Paris and place themselves at the disposal of the French Government, or cut their way out north to the Channel Ports.

That the position was indeed critical can best be realized when, after the war, one learns that Von Kluck himself, commanding the 1st Army, was actually by noon the following day in Lassigny, some six miles to the left rear of the position held by the Brigade.

However, luckily the Brigade was not actually attacked, and at dusk succeeded in withdrawing across the river by the bridge at Sempigny where Major Green remained on outposts till the early hours of the next morning.

About 2 a.m. Major Green withdrew and, after a march **30th Aug.** of five miles, at dawn the two halves of the Battalion met once more, and it was for the first time possible to count the survivors of Le Cateau.

The hardships had been great, and Major Green had covered by road measurement upwards of fifty-seven miles during the four days, made the more weary by innumerable alarms which frequently disturbed what little rest there was to be had.

For his admirable work throughout these days Major Green received the D.S.O.

During this time Lieut. Dowling acted as adjutant to Major Green, who afterwards brought to the notice of Lieut.-Col. Le Marchant the good work done by, and the loyal support he had received from this officer.

30th Aug.   Soon after dawn the Battalion was joined by Major Green's half Battalion, and the retreat continued throughout the day by Carlepont, Bailly, Berneuil and Trosly-Breuil. Dusk found the Battalion across the Aisne and entering the Forest of Compiegne, Pierrefonds was reached about 11 p.m. The march of some fifteen miles, though broken by two long halts, during one of which there was little rest, as *A* and *B* companies were on outpost, was very wearisome with the heat of the day, lack of guides in the dark, a road remarkable for short but exceptionally steep hills and occasional alarms from patrols or supposed patrols of German cavalry in the forest.

This trying march showed the fine spirit which existed in the Battalion. More than one N.C.O., sturdier than his fellows, could be seen carrying the rifles of two or even three of the men of his platoon rather than that his men should fall out. In one company also the company ' charger ' was used as a pack animal, and loaded up with rifles of the company.

Late on in the afternoon Lieut. Mathews was sent off on a message and, missing his way, did not find the Battalion again till 3rd September.

On arrival, owing to smallpox in the village, the Battalion bivouacked in the streets in the southern end of the village underneath the Chateau. Rations were not issued till the early hours of the morning, so there was little sleep for the exhausted troops.

It was on this day that the IVth Division and the 19th Infantry Brigade were formed into the 3rd Corps under General Pulteney.

It is perhaps of interest to record that soon after crossing the Aisne, news of the naval engagement at Heligoland was passed down the line of march, and at the same time the well-known rumour of vast numbers of Russian troops having arrived in England.

AFFAIR OF 1st SEPTEMBER.

It was on this day that news came that the German Government considered that the revolver ammunition supplied to officers was contrary to the Hague Convention, and threatened reprisals on any officer taken prisoner with this ammunition on him. Whether the German Government was right or wrong the writer is not, of course, competent to express an opinion. At any rate, it resulted in officers strewing the neighbouring fields with their ammunition.

About 7 a.m. the Battalion [the Brigade being advanced **31st Aug.** guard to the Division] marched by hot and dusty lanes through the forest of Compiegne to St. Sauveur, a distance of twelve miles. St. Sauveur, a small village nestling in a glade underneath a steep hill on the western edge of Compiegne forest, was reached soon after 11 a.m. Owing to the difficulty of the country and the exhaustion of the troops, this flank march of the 3rd Corps was much delayed, and on arrival at St. Sauveur, instead of going on to Saintines, where it had been intended to billet, the Battalion was ordered to take up an outpost position facing north to cover the remainder of the Corps, which dribbled through until far into the night.

D Company (Major Green) was posted on the right of the position in the forest connecting with the Hampshires, and A Company (Capt. Clayhills) on the left of the D Company, B and C Companies being held in reserve in the south end of the village. Some confusion occurred during the afternoon owing to the 4th Middlesex (IIIrd Division) also taking up an outpost position at St. Sauveur. The matter was put straight by the brigade major, who instructed the 4th Middlesex to withdraw to the high ground immediately behind the village and form a support for the Battalion.

The night passed without incident, other than continual **1st Sept.** sniping, though little was it realized that during the hours of darkness the 4th German cavalry division had slipped through a gap in the British line in the forest only to meet at

Nery some four miles to the rear of St. Sauveur with the heroic defence of *L* Battery, R.H.A., at the same time as the Battalion was engaged at St. Sauveur. As a matter of fact Major Green twice during the night sent in reports that he had heard " the sounds of a considerable body of troops, probably cavalry, on the move in the forest." No doubt this was the march of the German 4th cavalry division. It is impossible to trace what happened to these reports. Could the position have been fully realized at Corps Headquarters, probably the fate of the German cavalry division would have been even more in-glorious than it was on the 1st September.

About 7 a.m. *D* Company (Major Green) became engaged with the mounted troops forming the left of the advanced guard of the German 2nd Corps. About the same time the most disconcerting gun-fire of the engagement of Nery was heard in the rear of the Battalion. Two platoons of *C* Company were moved up to the eastern end of the village near the church, as an attack appeared probable. This soon began with considerable shell fire on the village. The shooting was accurate and made the position unpleasant, but, as the guns were light, little material damage was done.

About 10 a.m. Brig.-Gen. Hunter Weston, anxious about his right flank, which was rather in the air, decided to with-draw the Battalion and the Hampshires. The Hampshires being on the most exposed flank went first. *D* Company (Major Green) was ordered to retire as soon as the Hampshires were clear, and then in succession *A* Company (Capt. Clayhills) and *C* Company (Lieut. Hopkinson).

Owing to the dense undergrowth in the forest communica-tion between the Hampshires and Major Green was exceedingly difficult. The result was that unknown to Major Green the Hampshires had withdrawn to the high ground south of St. Sauveur by about 11 a.m. Major Green's position by now had become critical, as he had been engaged with German cavalry to his front, right flank and right rear, and so thick was the forest that he was unable to find out what was happening. Shortly before noon the commanding officer of the Hampshires, who was going round to see that all his battalion had got away, met Major Green and informed him that his battalion had withdrawn some time before. Major Green therefore withdrew his company, moving along the lower slopes of the high ground behind the village, thus skilfully extricating his company from a very awkward position practically without loss. C.S.M. Ward and L/Sgt. Brennan, both of *D* Company, on this, as on many other occasions, showed themselves not only to be men of fine fighting spirit, but also to have a thorough command of their men. The latter was shortly after promoted sergeant.

A Company then withdrew down the village street and then *C* Company by the same route. The withdrawal of these companies, which were in a less exposed position than *D* Company, was carried out with little difficulty.

The Battalion then retired by the road to Vaucelles, making use of the wooded country, and then, under cover of the Rifle Bde., on to the high ground near Nery.

Near Vaucelles the Battalion was fired upon by the Rifle Bde., which mistook it for the German advanced guard. Luckily the mistake was discovered before any casualties occurred.

Although apparently the Germans were in superior numbers, and, in fact, the head of the 2nd Corps was only a few miles behind the cavalry, the attack on St. Sauveur was never pressed with great vigour, and, as the position held by the Battalion was strong with a good field of fire, except on the right flank which was in dense forest, the Battalion lost but one officer, Capt. Seabroke, wounded and prisoner, and thirteen other ranks killed and missing—practically all in *D* Company. Among them was Sgt. Nevin, one of the most promising of the younger N.C.Os. of the Battalion. He is buried in the churchyard at St. Sauveur. Capt. Seabroke, shot in the leg, was placed by the Germans in hospital in Compiegne. Subsequently it was unfortunately found necessary to amputate his leg.   He was released by the French on the recapture of that town a fortnight later.

Lieut.-Col. Le Marchant's withdrawal of the Battalion might well be cited as a model for such an operation, as it was not discovered until too late by the enemy when the Rifle Bde. and Somersets covering the retirement on the high ground above Vaucelles inflicted, according to German accounts, considerable losses.   At the same time it should be remembered that had *D* Company been commanded by a less experienced officer, the morning's work might well have ended very differently.   It was but one of several incidents in which Lieut.-Col. Le Marchant showed how well he knew the different capabilities of those he commanded, and the trust that he had in them to carry out his orders.

It is worthy of note that it was largely the sound of firing at St. Sauveur that caused the 4th German cavalry division, after being roughly handled at Nery, to hide in the wooded country for some thirty hours, neither daring to attempt to rejoin the German Army nor to interfere with the retreat of the 3rd Corps.

After reaching the high ground at Nery the Battalion took up a position, and the Rifle Bde. retired through the Battalion.   The Brigade then retired slowly across the open country in artillery formation for some twelve miles south. During this retirement the Battalion formed the infantry of the rear-guard behind a screen of the 4th Cavalry Brigade and divisional cyclists.   It billeted eventually in the village of Rozieres in a farm which had only two hours before been in German hands.

One fine incident at St. Sauveur should be mentioned. Lieut. Belchier, on returning from taking the order for the retirement of *A* and *D* Companies, had to ride back to battalion headquarters along the village street held by *C* Company, which had to remain in position till *A* and *D* Companies were clear.   Lieut. Belchier, noticing that the withdrawal of the troops was having a rather unsteadying effect on *C* Company, rode his horse at a slow walk down the length of the street to steady the men, though he was under heavy shell fire all the way. This gallant action immediately had the desired effect.

The Battalion transport this day left St. Sauveur about 6 a.m. with orders to go to Verberie, but when on the Vaucelle–Verberie road hearing rifle fire to the north and north-east, and seeing the transport of the 12th Brigade take to the open country in a westerly direction, followed it. Eventually it struck the Verberie–Baron road some three miles south-west of Verberie, and turned south with orders to go to Baron.

Just before reaching this place it suddenly saw a small column of mounted troops in close order about eight hundred yards to the east moving parallel to it. The transport prepared for action, and was about to open fire, when a staff officer (thinking the column might be French) forbade this. There can be little doubt, however, that they were really part of the 4th German cavalry division, and a golden opportunity was missed, as by this time these troops had no fight left in them, and would have provided an easy victory. As it turned out, this German column was a few minutes later scattered by rifle fire from the woods north-east of Baron by other British troops.

Baron was reached late in the afternoon, and the transport then moved two miles north again to rejoin the Battalion at Rozieres.

At 2 a.m. Brig.-Gen. Hunter Weston moved the Brigade **2nd Sept.** out of the village, which in daylight would have been a regular shell trap, and the Brigade marched to a wood on the outskirts of the village, and there halted for three hours, when the retreat was ordered to be continued to Dammartin. The Brigade not being on the Dammartin road was therefore turned about and marched *via* Montagny to Eve, which was reached at 10 a.m. (ten miles).

The transport moved rather earlier than the Battalion,

and reached Dammartin about 10 a.m.   After a long halt
there Lieut. MacMullen heard that the Battalion was at Eve,
and so marched north again and rejoined the Battalion early
in the afternoon.

The Battalion rested in a large farm in the village till
7 p.m., when *A* and *C* Companies were ordered to take over
the outpost line held by the Rifle Bde. abreast the Montagny
road.   Late in the afternoon it appeared probable that the
Brigade would become engaged with the German Cavalry, as
the Rifle Bde. had seen their scouts.   French troops on the
left and the 1st Cavalry Brigade also reported their presence,
and it was rumoured that a considerable force was working
round the flank of the position.   In fact, Brig.-Gen. Hunter
Weston was in touch with the 1st Cavalry Brigade with a view
to co-operating in engaging these forces, but was ordered
by the IVth Division not to become involved in an action unless
necessary, as the Division was about to continue the retreat
southwards.   The outposts of the Battalion were not attacked,
though the sight of burning villages immediately to the north
confirmed the presence of the enemy.   In conformance with
the divisional order the outpost companies were withdrawn
at 10.30 p.m., and the march continued to Dammartin, with
the Battalion as rear-guard and *C* Company the rear party.

On reaching Dammartin there was considerable difficulty
in getting part of the brigade transport up the steep hill into
the village, and *C* Company was ordered by Brig.-Gen. Hunter
Weston, personally, to move north towards Eve to take up a
covering position till the Brigade cleared the hill.   The commander of *C* Company therefore retraced his steps towards
Eve, took up a position and waited, watch in hand, till the hour
of withdrawal as ordered by Brig.-Gen. Hunter Weston had
arrived.

3rd Sept.   The march continued *via* St. Mard and Annet to Lagny (on
the Marne).   Bivouac was reached in the Bois de Chigny (just
south of Lagny) about 1 p.m., after a march of eighteen miles,

in the course of which the Battalion passed through the outer defences of Paris, where French troops were hard at work.

During the march Lieut. Mathews, who had been missing since 30th August, rejoined the Battalion. This officer had found on returning from taking his message that the Battalion had disappeared, and not knowing in which direction it had moved off, had struck south, as every one in those days did when in difficulty, and eventually that night found troops of the 2nd Corps in the forest of Compiegne. With these he had remained till 3rd September, as until then he was unable to discover the whereabouts of his own battalion.

The day's march had been hot and trying but uneventful, as the duty of rear-guard had been taken over at St. Mard by the 19th Brigade.

Lieut. Hughes and a few men were left at St. Thibault near Lagny as an observation post, and did not rejoin the Battalion for three days.

C Company in the meanwhile had remained north of Dammartin till the hour at which its commander had been instructed by Brig.-Gen. Hunter Weston to withdraw. However, on reaching Dammartin just before dawn no sign of British troops was to be found, nor could any information be got from the few inhabitants who had not fled from the village nor had the company commander any maps to show the probable route taken by the Battalion. It is curious to reflect that only thirty hours earlier Dammartin had been the busy hub of General Headquarters of the British Army. After wandering about the village for some time a fork road was found with a signpost pointing to Paris on the most easterly of the two roads. Which road was to be taken was rather a problem, and the deciding point for the only two officers in the company was that a siege of Paris appeared probable, and that hence that was no place to make for. They therefore took the other which happened to be the route of the Division, and so eventually the company, after passing on the way through the 19th Brigade, which was considerably surprised to see it, overtook the Battalion a few miles north of Lagny.   The men arrived in a very exhausted condition as, in its efforts to regain touch with the Battalion, the company had marched from Dammartin to Lagny in nearly three hours less time than that taken by the Battalion.

The whole incident is, of course, trivial, but is a typical example of the dilemmas in which junior officers frequently found themselves during the Retreat.

4th Sept.   About 6.30 a.m. the Battalion moved to the Chateau Fontinelle some two miles away and rested in the grounds for the day, receiving for the first time since 26th August the services of a medical officer, who had a busy time looking after the feet of the men, many of whom could hardly have taken their boots off for ten days of continuous marching.   About 4 p.m. the Battalion marched four miles east to Coupvray, and *A* and *B* Companies took up an outpost position on the Canal.   About 10.30 p.m. the rest of the Battalion moved on to the high ground near Chalifert to reinforce the outpost companies, as it was rumoured that the Germans were advancing on the Marne.   The transport was sent back some four miles to Jossigny.   This advance proved unfounded as the main cause of the alarm, that the Germans were making a pontoon bridge higher up the stream, was proved untrue— the *débris* floating down the river being discovered to be drift wood !   So the Battalion had such peace as could be got on outpost duty.

5th Sept.   Early in the morning the outposts were withdrawn and the march continued, the Battalion being rear-guard to the Brigade.   About 3 p.m., after a long and trying march of close on twenty miles under a hot sun by Serris, Jossigny, and the Forest of Armainvilliers, the Battalion bivouacked in the grounds of Marsaudiere Chateau, about seven miles north of Brie Comte Robert, in a very exhausted condition.   It had been intended to reach Chevry, but owing to the exhausted condition of the men, the Battalion was ordered to halt some three miles north of Chevry. The transport had prepared the men's dinners at Chevry, and these were eventually brought by the transport to the bivouac of the Battalion. During the march the Battalion passed by the chateau Ferriers, the home of the Rothschilds, in which the Emperor William I. had stayed during the Siege of Paris in the Campaign of 1870. To the regimental officers who naturally knew nothing of the plans slowly being evolved by Gen. Joffre, it looked as if William II. was to follow in the footsteps of his grandfather.

Late that evening the " first reinforcement," Captain Preston and ninety-eight other ranks, arrived at Chevry, but even they were far from fresh as after a very long railway journey they had accomplished a march of thirty-five miles in twenty hours. Capt. Preston was posted to *D* Company.

The end of the retreat saw the Battalion reduced to twenty-two officers and about five hundred other ranks, one and all exhausted almost to the limit of human endurance. In abnormally hot weather, at the very commencement of a campaign, and with many reservists in the ranks, it had marched a hundred and fifty miles by road measurement during the ten days; and, of course, the distance covered by individuals must have greatly exceeded this. One pitched battle and several rear-guard actions, always against superior numbers, had been fought. It had frequently been on outposts, suffering innumerable alarms and excursions. Sleep had seldom been obtainable except by the roadside, and many a man had fallen asleep as he marched in the ranks. Food had often been scarce and always uncertain. Of medical aid there had been none. Even senior officers had frequently had no map to guide them. Was it to be wondered that the weight carried by the British soldier had proved intolerable, and that great coats, packs and entrenching tools had frequently been thrown away by the roadside ? Whenever engaged with the enemy the Battalion had held its own, and only been forced to retire by vastly superior numbers, yet day after day the march had always been backwards and seemed to have no ending. This, perhaps naturally, gave rise to a rather depressed feeling among officers and men. Moreover, wrapped up in local troubles and little knowing of other equally heroic sacrifices, confidence in our allies was on the wane. Nothing was known of the war as a whole, and so, although all ranks felt all would come right in the end, there was a distinct feeling that it had not done so up to date.

Yet the regimental tradition, peace-time training and mutual trust between officer and man, proved sufficient not only to prevent those acts of indiscipline which marred that other great retreat of the British Army to Corunna, but also to enable the Battalion to retain its fighting spirit, to play its part in the great battle which, all unknown to it, was to follow, and to march over eighty miles during the next seven days.

Some idea of the strain endured may be gained when we realize that the average amount of sleep for an officer during this period of eleven days works out at rather under four hours each day. It was this lack of sleep which had exhausted the Battalion perhaps more than anything else.

At the end of the Retreat F.M. Sir John French expressed his appreciation of the work of the IVth Division under Gen. Snow as follows :

" I have been wanting to meet you, your Brigadiers and C.Os., to enable me to tell them how much I appreciate the splendid work of all ranks of the IVth Division during the past ten days. I consider you saved the situation, and I look upon it as one of the finest bits of work ever done by the British Army."

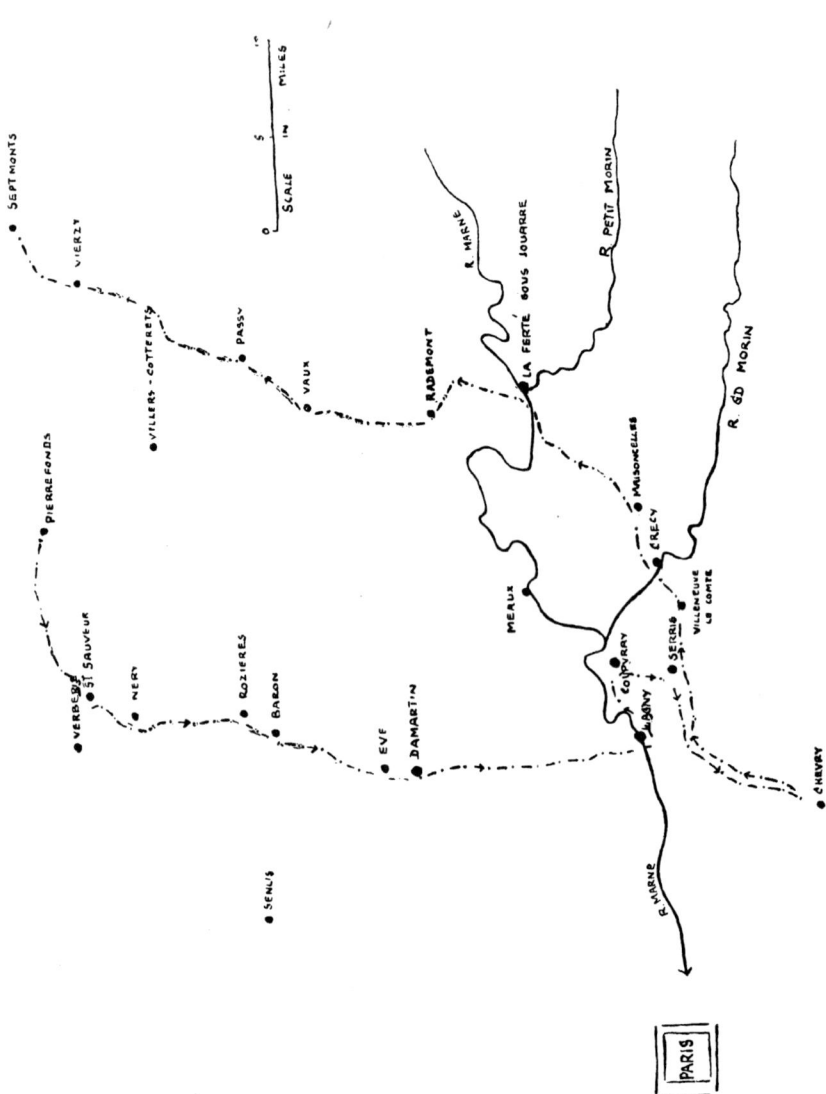

The Battalion paraded soon after dawn, but the march was not begun till about 7 a.m. Orders announced that the retreat had ended, but so utterly weary were the men that this produced no especial enthusiasm, and, as a matter of fact, was greeted by the Battalion with incredulous amusement, being thought to be but one of the numerous attempts to cheer up the troops that had been made during the previous days, and which had been all proved to have no foundation.

After a march of seventeen miles, *via* Jossigny, a bivouac was reached near Villeneuve le Comte about 1 p.m., and on arrival two platoons of *C* Company were detailed as outposts. During the march Lieut. Hughes and his detachment rejoined. What happened to this officer during the three days is not known. He arrived with the socks showing through his boots after the days of hard marching, and in this condition had to carry on for some time.

By 3 a.m. the Battalion was again ready for the road, but the march did not actually commence till 9 a.m. The heat was excessive and the Battalion marched on in absolute ignorance of the general military situation. *C* Company formed the advanced guard, and there was no map available for even the advanced guard commander. It was quite unknown to the officers of the Battalion whether there were British troops in front or whether German opposition was likely to be met at any moment.

On reaching Crecy on the Grand Morin about 11 a.m. the advanced guard overtook the rear of the Divisional Artillery, and it was therefore concluded that this additional labour for the men was unnecessary, and the advanced guard was withdrawn.

The march was continued to Maisoncelles which was reached late in the afternoon, and the Battalion halted by the roadside. Although nothing was known of the situation, it was at any rate recognized that the march had been an advance and not a retreat, a fact which considerably revived the spirits of the men.

Lieut. O. L. Wilson (R.A.M.C.) (temporary) reported for duty as medical officer to the Battalion, and a few odd men rejoined who had got lost on the Retreat and drifted into Paris and even further south.

Shortly before dusk Lieut.-Col. Le Marchant with *D* and *C* Companies moved off to take up an outpost position, but such was the general vagueness of the situation that it could not, with certainty, be determined which way the outposts were to face, or whether friend or foe lay to their supposed front.

Eventually the two companies settled down for rather an uneasy night facing east, astride what they had been informed was " a very dangerous road." That this was said to be " a very dangerous road " was all that was known of the military situation. Soon after dark gun-fire was heard not far to the front. This was followed by the hurried retirement of British transport down the road from the unknown, through the outpost line into Maisoncelles. Further, the sight of bivouac fires to the front, whether British or German, being impossible to be determined, only made the position the more obscure.

8th Sept.   Shortly before dawn mechanical transport gaily moved from Maisoncelles through the outpost line down the " very dangerous road," and at dawn artillery took up battle positions immediately in front of the outposts.

At 8 a.m. the Battalion continued the march. In the early afternoon small columns of British Infantry could be seen moving across country in " artillery formation," and as an occasional wounded man was met it was deduced that the enemy could not be far away. The Battalion, therefore, took to the open country, and in column of route plodded on its weary way, under cover of hedges and dead ground. Artillery in battle positions were passed and, after two long halts in a heavy thunderstorm, the Battalion, passing through Signy Signets eventually reached Les Corbiers farm on the

high ground above La Ferte-sous-Jouarre, about 6 p.m.
The Battalion billeted in this farm and an issue of cider, found
on the premises, did much to revive the men after a tedious day.

During this day the leading troops of the IVth Division
drove the Germans across the Petit Morin, and by dusk held
all that part of La Ferte-sous-Jouarre which lies south of the
river Marne.

At 3.30 a.m. the Battalion moved off along the road to 9th Sept.
La Ferte-sous-Jouarre, and as the day broke was going down
the steep hill into the south-west part of the town in column
of route on a road enclosed by cottages and gardens. Suddenly
the Battalion came under considerable machine-gun fire from
the houses on the north bank of the Marne. Taken completely by surprise the two leading Companies B (Capt.
Coventry) and C (Lieut. Hopkinson) scattered precipitately
into the nearest gardens, but after a few minutes were rallied
without difficulty by their officers. Luckily the German fire
was not accurate, and though the upper walls of the houses
were bespattered by a stream of bullets, no actual casualties
were suffered. It is impossible to say if Lieut.-Col. Le
Marchant had received any information which would have
led him to think his Battalion might come under fire so early.
The balance of probability seems to be that he had not, but
be that as it may, it was an unhappy beginning for the day,
and one which considerably affected the morale of the men.*

Taking greater precautions the march was continued to
the lower part of the town which lies in a narrow valley between
two steep hillsides covered with houses on both banks of the
river, which is about seventy yards broad.

Before moving down D Company (Major Green) was sent
to take up a position suitable for covering fire on the high
ground to the south-west of the town, where they remained
all day.

*The Brigade War Diary states that an officers reconnaissance had, before the
Brigade moved off, reported that the routes to the town were all clear.

After crossing the Petit Morin the Battalion halted near the Chateau at the cross-roads in the south of the town between the two bridges, both of which were completely destroyed.

The south bank of the river was found to be held by the Royal Welsh Fusiliers, who had already suffered considerable casualties. This regiment was withdrawn about 7.30 a.m. and, relieved by *A* and *B* Companies (Capts. Clayhills and Coventry), the former taking the left and the latter the right of the line.

C Company was held in reserve on the Montmirail road five hundred yards south of the chateau, which became Battalion Headquarters.

Capt. Goldie and Lieut. Delmege were sent to see if a crossing could be effected near the bridge in the north of the town, but this was impossible, and no progress could be made anywhere owing to the determined rifle and machine-gun fire from the houses and gardens of the north bank.

For the rest of the morning the position remained unchanged, though there was continual sniping along the river bank, and *D* Company at long range worried the German defence.

At 10.30 a.m. Lieut.-Col. Le Marchant set off to visit Lieut. Leeson's post, and while there was instantaneously killed by one of the numerous German snipers, whose fire all day, from cleverly concealed positions in houses on the north bank, was remarkably accurate.

Major Lambert therefore assumed command, Major Green became second in command, and Capt. Goldie took over *D* Company.

About noon *A* and *B* Companies were withdrawn from the houses on the south bank of the river, while the north bank was shelled by two 4.5 howitzers for an hour, after which *A* and *B* Companies again occupied their old positions, but still no progress towards effecting a crossing could be made.

Early in the afternoon two Battalions of the 12th Brigade, who had spent the morning searching for an alternative crossing, followed later by the Rifle Bde. detached from the 11th Brigade, effected a crossing at a weir some three miles higher up the river, and this caused the German resistance to slacken.

At 2.20 p.m. Major Lambert was able to report that the western bridge end was sufficiently free from fire for a reconnaissance of the bridge to be made by the R.E. Capt. Coventry did not, however, succeed in clearing the eastern bridge end for some time after, as the Germans still stubbornly held on to the opposite bank in this quarter of the town.

About 3 p.m. Brig.-Gen. Hunter Weston determined to cross the Marne by boats, and a small flotilla of half a dozen boats and one old barge was collected in the Petit Morin near where the river joins the Marne. This could luckily be done without being observed by the enemy. The boats held about six men in each, and perhaps twenty could be got into the barge. While the boats were being collected German troops were still in occupation of the north bank of the Marne, and dispositions were therefore made to give covering fire for the boats as the crossing seemed certain to be opposed. The artillery was warned of Brig.-Gen. Hunter Weston's intention, so that it could shell the north bank, and two companies of the Hampshires with machine-guns took up a covering position on the south bank of the Marne just below the junction of that river with the Petit Morin. Major Lambert now took command of the force of East Lancashires and Hampshires involved in the crossing. C Company, which had been in reserve all the morning, was brought down to the place of embarkation and detailed to go across first.

Somewhat earlier the Brigade-Major of the 11th Brigade had informed the IVth Division that an attempt to bridge the river at La Ferté by pontoons was not likely to be successful. The IVth Division also received information in the early hours of the afternoon that the 2nd Corps might require assistance. Therefore about 3.45 p.m. Brig.-Gen. Hunter Weston was instructed by the IVth Division to delay his crossing for the time being. An hour later Brig.-Gen. Hunter

Weston was ordered to carry on with the crossing and establish a strong bridge head on the north bank. The preparations were therefore continued, but Major Lambert this time detailed *A* Company, under Capt. Clayhills, who had on many occasions shown himself to be an exceptionally fine officer, to cross first instead of *C* Company. *A* Company then began to cross in the boats rowed by R.E., and to the intense relief of all concerned the leading boats reached the far bank without a shot being fired. Thus the crossing turned out to be unopposed, but this does not detract from the gallant way in which the leading boats set out on what seemed to all a desperate venture.

A steady stream of boats then continued, though owing to the current of the river and the poor craft the crossing was most laborious. *C* Company followed *A* Company, and then two companies of the Hampshires without loss, except for one boat-load of Hampshires capsizing, and in the failing light two men were drowned.

This force then occupied the railway embankment some five hundred yards north of the river, the two companies of the East Lancashires being on the right of the line, and remained there for the evening. An order was apparently given to the force now on the north bank to gain touch if possible with the eastern bridge opposite Capt. Coventry's company. What happened to this order is not known; all that can be said is that it never reached *C* Company, which held the right of the line.

About 9 p.m. orders to capture the high ground above the town reached the force on the north bank of the river. The attack was to be carried out at dawn, it being then believed that the heights were held in force by the Germans, and, as a matter of fact, at that hour they still were held by the German rear-guard.

Late in the evening the R.E. began to bridge the river by pontoons, but this was not completed till the early hours of the following morning.

Lt.-Col. L. St. G. Le MARCHANT, D.S.O.

Major Lambert divided the available troops on the north bank of the river into three columns :—*

Left Column .. 2 Coys. Hampshires .. Objective Morintru
Centre Column.. A Coy. (Capt. Clayhills)
  E. Lancashires and one
  Coy. Hampshires .. ,, Le Lilon
Right Column .. C Coy. (Lieut Hopkinson)
  E. Lancashires .. ,, Bergette

In order to reconnoitre the first part of the three routes, three officer patrols were sent out under Lieuts. Leeson, Canton and Mathews. The first two returned by midnight reporting all clear as far as they had gone. Lieut. Mathews, who had the rather more tedious task of also reconnoitring the town, through the centre of which C Company had to pass, returned about the same hour with the same report.

The loss of Lieut.-Col. Le Marchant was deeply felt throughout the Battalion. He had gained the confidence of his officers by being invariably ready to listen to the troubles of even the most junior of them. No officer was afraid to ask his advice, knowing that a firm but kindly helping hand would be given him. His imperturbability under the heaviest fire, his refusal to become rattled when things were going wrong, and his complete disregard of his own safety had earned from officers and men a trust which was not only a source of infinite strength to those he commanded, but also to his brigade commander. Brig.-Gen. Hunter Weston, shortly before Lieut.-Col. Le Marchant's death, had selected him as the most deserving of the senior officers of the Brigade for the French decoration given for the Retreat, and his Legion of Honour was afterwards presented to his sister. He was also mentioned in despatches.

*The Battalion War Diary states that B Company was also in the right column, but this is an error; possibly the original order hoped also to employ B Company, but whatever happened the commander of C Company never heard that they were to join him, and as a matter of fact they did not, and remained for some time on the south bank of the Marne.

Nothing was more typical of his life than his death—seeing for himself how things were.

Lieut.-Col. Le Marchant was buried in the grounds of the chateau which was used as Battalion headquarters by the Regiment he had loved and served so well. Some years later his body was removed to the small Anglo-French cemetery at La Perouse, some five miles south of La Ferté, where it now lies.

It is interesting to record that the south bank of the river has in memory of this day had its name changed from Quai de Maime to Quai des Anglais.

Besides Lieut.-Col. Le Marchant the Battalion lost seventeen other ranks killed and wounded. All these belonged to *A* and *B* Companies. The German losses at La Ferté are not accurately known, but they were estimated by the inhabitants to be about seven hundred during the two days' fighting. During the day a draft of fifty-eight other ranks arrived under 2nd Lieut. Waud who was posted to *D* Company.

10th Sept. About 1 a.m. Lieut. Mathews went out a second time to try and find out if the road up the hill was clear. He returned about 3.15 a.m., after having shown considerable pluck in going on himself, with one man only, well up the hill, though the rest of his patrol were so exhausted that he had had to leave them behind.

At 3.30 a.m. the advance began, rather an anxious one, up roads enclosed by houses and gardens and only partially reconnoitred. Just at dawn all three columns reached the crest, only to find that the Germans some two hours before had retired from their positions.

The right and centre columns in turn when half-way up the hill were attacked and fired on in their rear by an Uhlan patrol, which had remained hidden in the town, and who later in the morning surrendered. The centre column under Capt. Clayhills drove off this patrol with little difficulty. But the right column, suddenly attacked in rear when on a road enclosed by high walls, and just at the time when all thoughts were concentrated on what was about to happen to the front, was thrown for a short while into considerable confusion. The determined efforts of this patrol to cut their way out of La Ferté deserve admiration, and that they did not ride right through *C* Company was principally due to the presence of mind and good shooting of Cpl. Lismore, who happened to be in the rear of the Company. This N.C.O., practically single-handed, drove off the patrol, inflicting casualties among them, while the Company was being reformed. For this and further good work in November, 1914, Cpl. Lismore received the D.C.M.

One prisoner was taken at Bergette—the first taken by the Battalion in the war.

No account of the crossing at La Ferté would be just without acknowledging the fine determination and good fighting of the German rear-guard—apparently the 4th Jäger battalion and some cavalry—at this place. Taking full advantage of a position well adapted by Nature for a rear-guard action they had for many hours delayed superior British forces and eventually escaped with small loss.

At 9 a.m. *D* Company, after crossing the Marne by the pontoon bridge, passed through *C* Company at Bergette. About 11 a.m. the Battalion was concentrated once more on the La Ferté–Montreuil road, and in brigade marched north-west to Rademont, a village about eight miles north of La Ferté, being considerably cheered up on the way by seeing the *débris* of the German retreat on the roadside, in spite of the heavy rain which fell off and on throughout the day, drenching the troops to the skin. In Rademont the Battalion billeted in a particularly dirty farm, which was the more uncomfortable, as it had also been effectually looted by the Germans

The pursuit was continued by the Battalion in brigade 11th Sept. *via* Vendrest and Coulombs to Vaux, which was reached about noon, French troops being passed on the way. Near Vaux the Battalion halted till 3 p.m., when the march was continued to Passy, and on arrival about 5 p.m. went into billets. The day's march had been some eighteen miles, latterly in heavy rain along country lanes churned into seas of mud.

12th Sept. As usual the Battalion was warned to be prepared to march about 5 a.m., and, as usual, the march did not actually begin till some two to three hours later.

Marching *via* Marizy and Chouy the Battalion reached Villers-Helon about noon, where it remained till about 4 p.m. listening to considerable gun-fire as the French advanced on the left during the wet morning. In column of route the Battalion then moved on to Vierzy where preparatory battle formation was taken up, and the march was continued to Septmonts, which was not reached till 7 p.m. in heavy rain. The arrival of the Battalion at Septmonts cannot better be described than in the graphic but ungrammatical words of the Battalion war diary, " Full of transport and rain."

Few arrangements had been made for billeting the troops in the crowded village, and even these broke down completely. The first two hours were spent by the Battalion moving into billets and being ordered out again into the rain. Eventually the Battalion found a home in the church and a farm near by, where, in spite of the most determined efforts by other units, they succeeded in holding their ground against all-comers.

These additional hardships at the close of a wet and tiring day much reduced the spirit of the Battalion, so that, when parading some two hours later to continue the advance, even the really witty sally by one of the men in the church, " We will now sing ' Onward Christian Soldiers ' " produced not a ripple of laughter.

During the evening Brig.-Gen. Hunter Weston learned that the bridge over the Aisne at Venizel some three miles north of Septmonts, had not been completely destroyed, and that the north bank of the river itself was very lightly held by the Germans. Army orders issued late on the 11th had ordered the crossings of the Aisne to be seized as soon as possible. About 11 p.m., therefore, in spite of the exhaustion of his brigade after a trying march of eighteen miles, Brig.-Gen. Hunter Weston continued the advance, the Battalion forming the rear battalion of the brigade.

The valley of the Aisne is of a different nature from 13th Sept. that of the Marne, as there are two miles of flat meadow land between the southern and northern heights. The river itself flows at Venizel some sixty yards broad immediately under the southern heights. The river, it is true, was known to be but lightly held, but there was no definite information as to the enemy's strength upon the northern heights.*

To decide to assault these heights at dawn with troops already exhausted by a long march, little rest and less food, was therefore a bold conception, as, once over the river, uncrossable except by the half-broken bridge at Venizel, the brigade would be unable to receive support from the rest of the Army. On the other hand, this crossing of the open valley by a night march saved the Brigade having to do so in full view of the enemy the following day. The risk was great, but, as it turned out, was justified by the end attained.

By advancing on to the high ground above Bucy-le-Long, and not halting when he had seized the bridge at Venizel, Brig.-Gen. Hunter Weston showed himself to be an intrepid commander who, not content with merely carrying out his orders to the letter, did not hesitate to act further, so that they should be carried out to the spirit.

Amid sheets of rain and a howling gale the exhausted and dejected soldiery, to whom extra ammunition had been served out at Septmonts, fairly staggered over the hill and down to Venizel, not caring why or whither they went, driven only by the indomitable determination of their brigade commander.

* The divisional 4.7 battery had been brought into action with great difficulty just before dusk above Septmonts against retreating columns of the enemy on the hills north of the Aisne.

The river was successfully crossed and the leading battalions carried the crest above Bucy-le-Long by a bayonet charge at dawn, surprising the Germans who no doubt thought it impossible for the British pursuit to close on them so soon. Shortly before dawn the Battalion crossed at Venizel. The roadway of the bridge still held, it is true, but a main girder had been destroyed, and it could only be crossed in single file at two paces interval. As soon as the Battalion had crossed the bridge the rather hazardous job of getting the ammunition limbers across was successfully accomplished. The ammunition was taken out of the limbers and carried by hand, and the horses unhooked and the limbers manhandled over the bridge.

Lieut. Dowling's platoon was left behind at Venizel to guard the bridge. It rejoined the Battalion the next day.

About 7 a.m. the Battalion reached Bucy and took charge of a considerable number of prisoners captured by the leading battalions.

At 8 a.m. *C* Company (Lieut. Hopkinson), and at 10 a.m. *D* Company (Capt. Goldie) were moved up to support the Somersets, who were hanging on to the edge of the plateau above the village. During the morning these Companies were shelled but suffered small losses. By 1 p.m. the shelling stopped, and the rest of the day was spent watching the 12th Brigade crossing the valley at Venizel. Line upon line of men very widely extended advanced under heavy shell fire, as if on parade to the admiration not only of the British but also, from German accounts, of the enemy.

There was but one more incident that morning and that almost comic. So little was there known of the German position that Major Green with *A* Company (Capt. Clayhills) was sent off with orders to capture Fort Condé on a spur some three miles east of Bucy. On approaching the spur he found it held in great strength, and, being also under shell fire from his own guns south of the Aisne, decided it was hardly a suitable place to assault with one weak company, and so halted. Shortly after the 12th Brigade arrived on the same mission, but with the same result. The following day it was attacked by considerable British forces, but no impression was made on it. In fact, it was not captured till three years later !

And thus ended the first phase of the war—the Retreat and the Advance. Except for the short advance in October on the arrival of the Battalion in Flanders, the Battalion was not to be again engaged in moving warfare till 1918.

The Retreat had been carried out during an exceptionally hot August; the Advance during an exceptionally wet September, and the latter, owing to the shortage of equipment, was all the harder on the troops. During the Retreat and the Advance only one instance of drunkenness occurred in the Battalion—at Passy.

During the three weeks that the Battalion was on the Aisne at Bucy-le-Long it was never heavily engaged, though it often took part in minor actions and was shelled at frequent intervals.

The Brigade held the edge of the plateau above the village and no serious attempt was made by the Germans to force it back over the river. In fact, by virtue of its night march the Brigade was in a considerably happier position than most units in the British Army.

It was perhaps lucky that the Germans did not seem to realize, or, if they did, were unable to exploit the precarious position held by the Brigade. The line held was very extended, and as a result the Brigade reserve was often very small.

Owing to the configuration of the ground no field artillery support could be given to the infantry except by howitzers. One battery of howitzers was in position for the first few days in the field immediately north of the church at Bucy-le-Long, but was soon shelled out of it and retired to the south bank of the river, where it was unable to support the Brigade owing to the long range. Therefore there was no artillery support available except the divisional 4.7 heavy battery, which was on the ridge north of Septmonts. It is true that a section of field artillery was, towards the end of the time, placed actually in the front line, but this could only be used as a last resort for close action in a limited area.

For the first ten days the Battalion was much broken up as companies had been sent up piecemeal to reinforce the front line of the Brigade as needed. Many minor moves of companies were made. It is hardly necessary to record the details of these company movements. The front line was a patchwork of all battalions of the Brigade. In general, Battalion headquarters with A and C Companies were on the left of the line north-west of Bucy, and B and D Companies on the right of the line north of the village. The Battalion machine-guns were in the road leading north from Bucy to Anizy. Battalion headquarters were first in a cave (since blown in) on the spur. Later, owing to the dampness of the cave, dug-outs were made slightly lower down the spur.

The Battalion was thus the left-hand battalion of the British Army in touch with the French 6th Army.

On 16th September Bucy-le-Long was heavily shelled by 8 in. howitzers. This was the first time the Battalion met really heavy artillery, and the name " Black Marias " came into use from the columns of black mud thrown up by the shells. It was a name later to be spoken of throughout the world. The transport was on this day lying in the village at the Mairie, and several men and horses were lost before it could be moved to a safer place. In this shelling C.Q.M.S. Smith was severely shell-shocked. He had by his intelligence and long experience been of the greatest assistance to his youthful officer on many difficult occasions during the Retreat. That the transport was not completely wrecked was largely due to the prompt and plucky handling of the situation by Lieut. MacMullen, who had already during the early days of the Retreat shown himself to be a most capable officer.

A platoon of Turcos, of the neighbouring French division, who were billeted with the transport, also suffered heavily. When the Battalion transport buried the Turco dead there was much speculation as to how they were to be placed—should their heads or feet face Mecca, and in what direction did Mecca lie with regard to Bucy ? Eventually a compromise was made, and their heads faced the Mairie in Bucy.

This Turco platoon, when they first arrived out of the unknown, caused considerable excitement amongst the men of the transport, as, on arrival, their sergeant, in order no doubt to impress the British, gave a sort of juggling display with a string of most gruesome human trophies from the battle of the Marne. This was too much for the transport officer, who promptly sent them off to Brigade H.Q. with a note saying,

"Herewith 50 Turcos." But they were not so easily disposed of, for they shortly after came back proudly showing a message from the Brigade Major, no word of which they of course understood : " Herewith 50 Turcos returned for your retention." So they stayed and eventually became good friends of the Battalion, as they and their successors subsequently lived in the Battalion line, though their lack of sanitary arrangements were a continual source of worry to the Battalion.

The transport nightly went to Septmonts for rations, remaining in Bucy for the day as the road across the valley was liable to heavy shelling in day time, being in full view of the hostile artillery.

Thus at last the Battalion not only received regular rations, but also could locally supplement these. The officers' mess actually kept a pen of ducks, fowls and rabbits outside their dug-out. The local bakery was got going, and issued bread to the civilian population and troops in regulated amounts. One day the Battalion ran short of bread, but found that all bread for the troops had been issued except for Brigade headquarters. However, the resources of the Battalion were not exhausted. The situation was explained to Emile, the French interpreter, attached to the Battalion. He proved himself to be a man of resource, as he promptly went down to the bakery demanding " Bread for the English General " and brought it back to the Battalion. What happened when the Brigade mess demanded their rations at the bakery is unknown—perhaps just as well.

The only serious alarm of an attack on the position was on the night of the 21st September, and a few men were lost in reinforcing the front line.

On 24th September forty stragglers rejoined the Battalion. These were men who had got lost during the Retreat, and had been absorbed by other units. The Battalion on its part shed some two dozen men of other units which it had absorbed, the procedure being that stragglers were sent back to divisional headquarters with the transport (with a chit showing the length of service they had had with the Battalion), and then going up to their own unit with its transport.

Most of the time was spent by the Battalion in improving the front line by night and the communications to the rear by day. Latterly a complete trench line was dug from the spur north-west of Bucy to the Aisne, in case the French were driven back on the left. It was the forerunner of the " switch " system of defence, and the prevision shown by Brig.-Gen. Hunter Weston in ordering this line to be dug was proved when the whole Crouy–Bucy position was lost by the French in January, 1915. The fact that the French failed after the loss of Crouy to hold the switch in no way detracts from Brig.-Gen. Hunter Weston's fore-thought.

Entertainment was afforded to the troops by watching the daily shelling of the French field battery in position below the spur. This battery, though continually in action, was never discovered, though a dummy battery in the next field was daily smashed to pieces and nightly repaired. The un-limited ammunition for this battery was a source of wonder to the British—it seemed inexhaustible, and any British officer who went down to the battery had only to ask " how the guns worked," and the battery at any hour of the day would im-mediately come into action for his benefit, firing diagonally against the German position at Crouy, which was frequently but unsuccessfully attacked with the greatest gallantry by the French native troops, and whose wounded often crawled back into the Battalion line.

One night some officers of the French battery and the neighbouring infantry escort were dined in the mess. It promised to be a good evening, but hardly came up to expecta-tions. In the first place, the wine, especially bought for the occasion, turned out to be a sticky syrup, and before the evening was over the French officers had to depart hurriedly, as heavy firing broke out in their lines. It was afterwards found out that the French native troops, bored with the inactivity of a fortnight's trench warfare, had, in the absence of their officers, elected to enliven the situation by carrying out an assault on the German position on their own, which, unfortunately, resulted in heavy losses.

During the stay at Bucy equipment was issued to replace that which had been lost during the Retreat, and, taking advantage of the comparative peace, rapid progress was made towards recovery from the trials and consequent disorganization of the Retreat. On 19th September Lieut. Warner and a draft of eighty-three other ranks joined. This officer was posted to *B* Company. Capt. Cane joined the Battalion on 26th and was posted to *B* Company. On 26th September Maj.-Gen. Rawlinson, at that time in temporary command of the IVth Division, inspected the trenches of the Battalion. On 1st October the Battalion (except the machine-guns, which remained in their position) was at last concentrated and acted as reserve to the Brigade on the spur north-west of Bucy. About 1st October Lieut. Hughes and thirty men were sent back to Septmonts to act as divisional headquarter guard. Each battalion had in turn found this guard which was utilized as an opportunity to give a rest to those who most needed it. During the stay on the Aisne the Battalion got news of the outer world for the first time since leaving England. It was in this wise : Col. Seely, on the staff of F.M. Sir John French, one day came over to look at the line and was given tea in the mess. In return he asked what he could send us, and the answer was a newspaper. Sure enough, a bundle arrived by car the following day—a thoughtful act.

On 27th Divine Service was held on the lower slope of the spur behind Battalion H.Q. It was chiefly memorable for the text chosen, " I will lift up mine eyes unto the hills from whence cometh my help." Naturally all eyes were turned heavenwards ; only to see a German aeroplane spotting for their artillery. Not long after the " help " did indeed come, but was far from comforting.

On 1st October Lieut.-Col. Lawrence come out from the

Depôt and assumed command of the Battalion. Major Lambert reverted to second in command again, Major Green to *D* Company, and Capt. Goldie to *C* Company.

During the short period during which Major Lambert had commanded the Battalion he had proved himself to be in every way a worthy successor to Lieut.-Col. Le Marchant. His firm but kindly discipline had done much to enable the Battalion to recover from the effects of the Retreat. Both as second in command and commanding officer he had invariably shown the same characteristics as Lieut.-Col. Le Marchant—a strong sense of discipline, yet tempered with kindness to those under him, utter fearlessness for his own life, and a determination to uphold the great traditions of the Regiment.

Few battalions in the Army can have had two finer men and better soldiers as their commanding officers than did the 1st East Lancashire Regiment in August and September, 1914. Major Lambert commanded a division in the later stages of the war and was killed in Ireland during the Sinn Fein troubles after the war.

Towards the end of September F.M. Sir John French **5th Oct.** proposed to Gen. Joffre that the British Army should move to the north of France. This was agreed to by Gen. Joffre, and the transfer of the British Army began. The Battalion was relieved by the French shortly before dusk and marched to Septmonts. Before leaving the Aisne position XXX was cut in the rock above Battalion Headquarters. This still clearly remains though difficult to find in the dense undergrowth, and, even the trenches made by the Battalion were still in existence in 1926. *A* Company this night were on outposts covering Divisional Headquarters.

Shortly before leaving the Aisne blankets were issued to the troops. They were much appreciated by the men, as many of them had no great coats. To carry these blankets the Battalion was given two local wagons, and drivers for these were sent back to Septmonts to undergo a short course of French horse management, as it had been discovered that French horses did not always understand the methods of driving and words of endearment and encouragement in use in the British Army. It is to be regretted that no details of this course are known. They would no doubt be amusing.

6th Oct. At 4.45 p.m. moved to Carriere l'Eveque farm above Septmonts. R.S.M. Ebsworth and C.S.M. Stanley were dined in the officers' mess on being offered their commissions. The former refused his commission but accepted one later on and was eventually killed in 1918 as an acting Lieut.-Col. in command of the 9th Northumberland Fusiliers, after having previously won the Military Cross; the latter accepted and was killed in November, 1914.

2nd Lieut. Lewis and 2nd Lieut. Palmer joined with a draft of about 100 other ranks. These officers were posted to *A* and *D* Companies respectively.

7th Oct. Marched at 10.30 a.m. and bivouacked at Buzancy Chateau at 12 noon. At 11.30 p.m. the march began again.

8th Oct. The Battalion arrived at Billy-sur-Ourcq at 3.45 a.m. and marched again at 5 p.m., passing through Villerets-Coterets late in the night.

9th Oct. Billeted at 1 a.m. at Largny and marched again at 1.30 p.m. to Bethisy-St. Pierre, arriving at 7 p.m.

Marched at 2 p.m. and arrived about 7 p.m. at Compiegne **10th Oct.**
after passing through St. Sauveur—the village the Battalion
had held on 1st September.

Late in the evening the Battalion entrained for Flanders.

OFFICERS OF THE BATTALION ON ENTRAINING FOR FLANDERS.

LIEUT.-COL.	G. H. LAWRENCE	Commanding Officer
MAJOR	T. S. LAMBERT	2nd in command
MAJOR	J. E. GREEN	D company
CAPT.	E. E. COVENTRY	B ,,
CAPT.	G. CLAYHILLS	A ,,
CAPT.	A. ST. L. GOLDIE	C ,,
CAPT.	L. A. F. CANE	B ,,
CAPT.	T. H. PRESTON [S.R.]	D ,,
LIEUT.	J. F. DYER	Machine Guns
LIEUT.	F. D. HUGHES	D company
LIEUT.	H. M. WARNER	B ,,
LIEUT.	E. C. HOPKINSON	C ,,
LIEUT.	F. E. BELCHIER	Adjutant
LIEUT.	W. E. DOWLING	C company
LIEUT.	E. M. B. DELMEGE	B ,,
LIEUT.	N. A. LEESON	A ,,
LIEUT.	H. T. MACMULLEN	Transport
LIEUT.	H. W. CANTON	A company
LIEUT.	C. E. M. RICHARDS [S.R.]	D ,,
2ND LIEUT.	W. T. TOSSWILL	A ,,
2ND LIEUT.	T. H. MATHEWS	C ,,
2ND LIEUT.	R. Y. PARKER	B ,,
2ND LIEUT.	L. D. WAUD	D ,,
2ND LIEUT.	F. E. G. LEWIS	D ,,
2ND LIEUT.	G. H. STANLEY	C ,,
2ND LIEUT.	R. W. PALMER [S.R.]	D ,,
2ND LIEUT.	G. H. T. WADE [S.R.]	B ,,
HON. LIEUT.	R. LONGSTAFF	Quartermaster
LIEUT.	O. L. WILSON [R.A.M.C. temp.]	Medical Officer

Of these during the fighting in October and November, 1914, Capts. Coventry, Clayhills, Cane and Preston, Lieuts. Warner, Mathews, Hughes, Waud and Stanley were killed.

Majors Lambert and Green, Capt. Goldie and Lieut. Hopkinson were wounded.

Lieuts. Dowling, Delmege, Longstaff and Wilson were invalided sick.

Two appreciations of the good work done by the Battalion may be quoted to show it had not been in vain.

On giving up command of the 11th Brigade in January, 1915, Brig.-Gen. Hunter Weston wrote of the Battalion : " They had always been reliable : they had died but never given way, and they had acted up to the highest traditions of the British Army. There could be no higher praise."

Field-Marshal Von Kluck, when meeting for the first time after the war a General officer of the old British Army, said to him : " In the whole history of the world there is in my opinion no military feat which has ever been excelled or equalled by that accomplished by the British Army in 1914. My admiration for that Army is greater than I can express."

Both, it should be mentioned, refer also to the desperate defence of Le Gheir in October to November, 1914, as well as to the deeds recorded in this book.

To add further praise is not necessary. Sufficient is it to say that the Battalion had honourably maintained the high traditions and proud record won in every quarter of the globe during the two hundred years of its existence. Fresh laurels had been added to be emblazoned on the Regimental Colours—honours which are not only a memory of a great past, but which should also serve as an incentive to a yet greater future.

F

TABLE SHOWING DAILY DISTANCES MARCHED BY
THE BATTALION.

Aug.	24th	6	miles
,,	25th	7	,,
,,	26th .. Battle of Le Cateau ..	—	
,,	27th	30	,,
,,	28th	15	,,
,,	29th	5	,,
,,	30th	15	,,
,,	31st	12	,,
Sept.	1st	12	,,
,,	2nd	10	,,
,,	3rd	18	,,
,,	4th	8	,,
,,	5th	19	,, (end of the Retreat)
,,	6th	17	,,
,,	7th	10	,,
,,	8th	10	,,
,,	9th .. Battle of the Marne ..	—	
,,	10th	10	,,
,,	11th	18	,,
,,	12th	22	,, (crossing of the Aisne)

The above is by map road measurement and takes no account of the minor marches of individual companies to take up outposts, etc., which must have greatly increased the total distance.

Major T. S. LAMBERT.

Future generations may perhaps wonder what was the mental outlook of the average private soldier as he went forth to war in August, 1914.

Patriotism, in the sense of a demonstrative love of country, might perhaps have seemed non-existent to the casual observer. The curious suppression of this feeling was not of course a trait of the professional soldier alone, but was a national characteristic. It no doubt existed deeper down. The Frenchman set out on his adventures to the martial strains of the " Marseillaise " and shouts of " La Patrie." But who could imagine an English battalion marching to " God save the King " ? Rather did they land in France to " Tipperary "— a second-rate song of the music-halls. Perhaps it was that the English soldier took it for granted that his patriotism was beyond suspicion. Whatever it was, he seldom allowed himself to express it, though his acts proved it to be there.

As to the Empire, it meant to the private soldier but little more than a string of stations, often reputed to have vile climates, which encircled the world.

Esprit de corps for Brigade or Division was almost negligible—a marked contrast to the strength this feeling attained later in the war. This lack of divisional *esprit de corps* was no doubt due to the circumstances under which the British Army served. Battalions were continually on the move and seldom remained in the same division for more than three years, and, indeed, were often at home and especially abroad in isolated stations.

On the other hand, *esprit de corps* from a regimental point of view ran exceptionally strong. The honour of his own regiment was the soldier's ideal, and, provided that this was upheld, little else mattered. Barrack room lectures on early battles had as a rule developed into little more than recounting the deeds of the Regiment.

Indeed, the regular Army was unfortunately in general a thing apart from, rather than part of the nation; though latterly some progress had been made towards bringing the two closer together through the Territorial Army.

This lack of national feeling in and for the Army was perhaps the result of one hundred years of freedom from invasion, as although during this period the professional Army had been ceaselessly engaged in every quarter of the globe, not one of its wars could be said to have directly affected the normal life of the nation. The outlook was perhaps narrow, but it was one which was at any rate to go far towards maintaining the tradition of the Regiment in the hard days to come, and also for the Regular Army to withstand the first onslaught, thereby giving time for the nation to put forth its full power.

The sentiments of the soldier can perhaps to some extent be shown by two incidents, the first at Colchester, the second at Havre. The first anecdote relates to a fatigue party at work at the station. While it was there, a rumour reached it that the Germans had landed on the East Coast. Some of the men came to the officer in charge of the party asking if the party could go back to barracks straight away. When asked why, they replied, " Oh ! they say the Germans have come, and if we don't go back the Regiment may go without us." That England had been, or rather was supposed to have been invaded did not worry them : what did, was that the Regiment might go into a fight without them.

The other was on the march from the docks to the camp at Havre. The night was hot and the hill long and steep. Early on, the troops sang on the march. "Tipperary" had been sung for heaven only knows how many times. Each time, as the hill grew steeper, in a rather more subdued key. At length it ended, to be followed by one of the Battalion wits with, " Why the hell carn't these —— Frenchmen fight their own —— battles " ?—a remark which was cheered to the echo.

The one grouse—and it is the British soldier's peculiarity that he continually grouses, and yet at the same time cheerfully does his duty—probably was that the football season was approaching, and it was feared that the first half of the season would be interfered with. Few, indeed, thought that the war would last long enough to interfere with the Cup Final of April, 1915. If among the men there was certainly no enthusiasm for, or understanding of the ideals for which they were to fight; on the other hand, there was much enthusiasm for a fight against whom or for what ideals it did not much matter.

A short reference to the feelings of the officers of the Battalion may be made. One and all had for some time been convinced that a war with Germany must come sooner or later, and it was therefore no surprise. The junior officers, not realizing " what they were in for " were all delighted at the prospect; the more senior officers, with not only the experience of South Africa but also a greater knowledge of the world, naturally appreciated more fully what a European war would mean.

Lightning Source UK Ltd.
Milton Keynes UK
UKOW051103290812

198205UK00001B/45/A